PICKING UP THE
SHARDS

Healing the Pain of Mother-Wounds,
Discovering the Mother-Heart of God

To,
Jeff

Blessings,
Anita

ANITA M. OOMMEN
Broken to Restored Series - Book 1

Picking Up The Shards. Healing the Pain of Mother-Wounds, Discovering the Mother-Heart of God.

Copyright © 2019 by Anita M. Oommen

Requests for information should be addressed to:
Oxborough Publishing, P.O. Box 815191, Dallas, TX 75381

ISBN: 978-1-7331115-0-8 (paperback)

All scripture quotations, unless otherwise indicated are taken from The Holy Bible, New International Version®, NIV® Copyright © 1973, 1978, 1984, 2011 by Biblica, Inc.® Used by permission of Zondervan. All rights reserved worldwide. www.zondervan.com.

The "NIV" and "New International Version" are trademarks registered in the United States Patent and Trademark Office by Biblica, Inc.®

Other Bible translations quoted in this book are listed in the "Bible Translations Cited" section.

Any internet addresses (websites, blogs, etc) and telephone numbers in this book are offered as a resource. They are not intended in any way to be or imply an endorsement by the publisher nor does the publisher vouch for the content of these sites and numbers for the life of this book.

Library of Congress Control Number: 2019905467

Published in association with Oxborough Publishing

Cover design: Heidi Sutherlin
Cover photo: Black and white childhood pictures & IMamarazzi Studios
Author photo: Katherine L. Wright, IMamarazzi Studios
Interior design: Matias Baldanza

First printing June 2019 / Printed in the United States of America

DEDICATION

To you—my beloved friend. Who has experienced the pain of Mother-Wounds, the deep loss of an earthly mother-child relationship that was meant to be yours but was stolen away too quickly… setting you up to wonder whether God had any idea what that was like or if he had any plans for you in letting you walk through the dark valley where you were wounded from abandonment, stung by rejection, and covered with the shroud of unworthiness by the very one you thought was supposed to nurture, love, and protect you in this world… I understand.

God has a Mother's Heart for you and he loves you with a patient, faithful, fierce, intimate, and compassionate love.

You are loved!

PRAISE FOR PICKING UP THE SHARDS

If you are ready to break the cycle of family dysfunction, *Picking Up The Shards* is the book for you! As a mental health nurse (for the past twenty-five years), I have seen the cycle of dysfunction tear through families. As a child of abuse, I related and connected with Anita as she shares her deepest feelings.

As you read her story, you can feel her pain and sense her strength at the same time. Her story helps you realize that you are not alone. She validates your feelings of past abandonment and neglect by confronting her own feelings in order to open doors to healing.

I would recommend this book to anyone ready to heal and put the pieces of their life back together.

—**Kelly Walk Hines,**
Best-selling Author *Memoirs of an Invisible Child*,
Recipient of the Heartland Hero Award by NJ Heartland

The best thing about Anita's book is that she is completely vulnerable. The traumatic experiences of her past help her relate to people on a personal level. As she has worked through her own attachment trauma and other childhood pain, she has become a beacon of hope and light to those struggling with the same thing. And she demonstrates all of this through her book.

—**Rachel Penning McCracken,**
Author, editor, *Chasing Kites Publishing*

It is this amazing book… a Memoir… it is so raw and real. It is beautifully done… I am in her target audience. I've been through so much of what she has been through, it was so relatable. It was such a healing experience for me.

—**Qat Wanders,**
Best-selling author, editor, *Wandering Words Media*

CONTENTS

~☙

FOREWORD BY MARCY PUSEY

W hen Anita asked me to write this foreword for her book, I was truly honored. Having been Anita's writing coach, I've had a front-row seat to her journey with this book's topic. As I tell most of my writing students, I prepared her for the ways that the writing of one's story often leads to new and fresh experiences with the topic at hand. If a writer is tackling a book on overcoming depression, they might get hit with the worst case of depression they've ever experienced. If they're writing the top ten ways to find financial success, they might find themselves in a financial bind. God seems to allow us a fresh opportunity with our stories and our lessons in order to tell them as truthfully as possible. This was no less true for Anita.

In Anita's case, writing about mother-wounds and the mother-heart of God led her to some deep, surprising, internal places. She found valleys and alleys long forgotten that were all due for a visit. Life took twists and turns in her own mothering and in her relationship with mother figures. And in the final days of preparing this book, her dear father passed away, paving new pathways of understanding, healing, and growth in her relationships.

Because of all she's experienced, Anita is one of the bravest, most steadfast, humble, dedicated people I know. She has held her hands wide open as she bore her heart, mind, and soul onto these pages for you. She has prayed for you, cried for you, and rejoiced for you, knowing that the comfort God has given her in her troubles will be a source of comfort to you in yours. Her vulnerability, authenticity, and invitation into her journey of discovery are all for you, sweet ones. I have watched her labor over every detail with the hope that you will find friendship within these pages. Even greater than friendship, a deeper relationship with a God who loves you with the unconditional, sacrificial love of a father, the fierce protection and compassionate tenderness of a mother.

I remember a moment on a women's retreat when I was desperately broken. My life felt like it had fallen into a million pieces. I was empty. Depleted. I had nothing left to give *and yet* I was a mother to four, wife, sister, daughter, and missionary. I'd been a helper, a do-er, and, unfortunately, an enabler. During one session, I happened upon one of the leaders. She saw my heartache and led me to a couch to talk. I ended up in shambles, with every bit of the ugly cry and nonsensical explanation. This sweet woman took my head and leaned me onto her shoulder. She stroked my hair and prayed over me. I wept all the harder. Now, I had a decent relationship with my mom. I've never thought of myself as having a mother-wound. But, at that moment, I found it. I found all the places my own mother just couldn't fill. Didn't fill. The God-shaped mother-holes that

I'd buried with good deeds and busyness. In that moment, God showed me that I had a longing for a mama to hold me in her lap and tell me it would all be okay. God's mother-heart expressed through this precious, willing woman.

Anita's book is like that. Like the woman who took my broken heart and filled me with God's love and hope, *Picking Up The Shards* acknowledges the hard and broken, then speaks to the beauty and joy of restoration. Each chapter, painfully and beautifully honest, ends with reflection questions and words of encouragement. Anita graciously points the broken-hearted toward healing. Don't miss this! The point of her story isn't the pain, but the healing that God brought to her broken places. The healing He longs to bring to yours. But without the pain, we miss the healing. Walk with her, as I've done, into the depths of her journey, but don't stop. Keep walking until you join her in the light and redemption on the other side.

So I entreat you to come to these pages just as you are. Whether you have visible wounds from your mother or invisible wounds, wounds you're aware of and wounds you're not, or no wounds at all—there's a place for you here. A place to experience the way God longs to hold you to his chest, stroke your hair as only a mama can, and swallow you up in safety, security, and the assurance that you are loved.

—Marcy Pusey, Certified Rehabilitation Counselor, author, speaker, and coach. Best-selling author of *Reclaiming Hope* and *Parenting Children of Trauma*.

Introduction:

⤳

MY ORPHANED HEART

I had just turned forty. Four decades of life. And my life's ground zero stared harshly back at me. In every sense, I was peering into the deep, dark abyss of a hopeless future—gazing into my imminent grave, buried alive by the mud of my past as it quickly closed in on me—physically, emotionally, and spiritually. Uncontrollable spasms in my stomach, a constant tight knot in my chest—all I wanted to do was curl up under the covers in a fetal position and never see the light of day again. With the fog in my head, I did not have space for God.

How did I arrive here? What went wrong? Did bringing children into this world take me down a dark forgotten path back into my childhood?

I walked into my counselor's office. With sage green walls and the scent of lavender from a candle on the end table in the waiting room, her office was inviting. The aroma that infused the air invigorated my senses. "Hello! You must be Anita," she said reaching out her hand to shake mine. Her face was kind and graceful, radiating delight and mercy. Five minutes into our conversation, I presented her with my discombobulated offerings. I told her that my head held two big signs: *"A"* for Abandonment and *"T"* for Trauma. Somehow, that is where I had arrived *AT*.

It was too hard for me to digest her words: *"orphaned heart."*

Was this just a crossroads? A midlife crisis? Or was this the realization of a dream that I had two decades before?

In my dream, I saw myself in a large field, the vastness of which almost encircled the ends of the earth. My eyes couldn't find its boundaries because they met the horizon. I looked around, seeing people from my life. They were at a distance, but just close enough I could recognize their faces. Friends, family, acquaintances, you name it, they were all there. I carried a basket in my hands, the contents of which were glass—broken glass. My basket was very heavy, and I wished someone would offer to help me carry the load. But why would they want to? Before I could process my thoughts any further, I dropped my basket. The already broken pieces spilled onto the ground and further broke into a million tiny shards of glass.

With tears streaming down my face, I knelt down and picked up every single one of those tiny pieces. It took what felt like an eternity. Once I had gathered them all back into the basket, I continued walking. The weight of the broken mess was too much to bear alone. My tired soul dropped the basket again and again until the pieces became much like dust.

Then I arrived at a tranquil, serene place which was made of glass—not pieces of glass but of *unbroken* glass. I so wanted to trade my broken shards, now a basket full of powdered glass, for something whole and unbroken. I saw myself receiving a *whole* glass slab; it wasn't difficult to hold. It was beautiful; it reflected such peace and serenity. I looked into it and found my two eyes—with a twinkle in them. My perspired face with darkly circled eyes faded in the light of the glimmer of hope I saw in my very own reflection.

Unexpectedly, I heard a loud voice, yet gentle and kind. Nudged to turn around, I looked into the vastness of the field that I had tirelessly journeyed through. I saw thousands of people—men, women, boys, and girls—from all walks of life, holding their baskets. As each of them made their way toward me, I stretched out my *whole* glass slab, on which I received their shards of glass and gave it to the "Eternal One"—the *One* who made me whole. In turn, He handed me unbroken slabs of glass that I was to deliver to each of these broken-hearted people.

I left this dream tucked away somewhere in the recesses of both my mind and soul. But now, in this inviting office, it finally began to make sense. In the valley of my grave, this dream, this memory, gave me a new glimmer of hope. Maybe, just maybe, it took this moment for my mess to meet my purpose—for me to *hope* again.

Was I entering into what some call a Divine calling, a revelation of sorts? Was I about to step into something bigger than myself, walking into my mess and finding my purpose in the dust, in the ground of the womb where I was created?

All I could think of at that very moment in my therapist's office was gut-wrenching, soul-writhing feelings of being orphaned and unseen by God and others. If there was a God, my family, my friends, and the people around me would reflect that in a tangible way—with their presence, their nurturing support, and by offering a listening ear to the cries of my soul. However, I did not feel anything remotely close to this. God seemed like a distant concept.

The therapist's office wasn't the first place I heard about being *orphaned*. I had a precious friend and mentor who spoke the truth with such grace about my life—my reality—that I didn't want to hear. I continued meeting with my therapist for the next nine months, but I was stuck in my healing journey. I hit a roadblock—I began re-experiencing trauma by reliving past wounds from my childhood and I just couldn't get beyond it. I couldn't put my finger on it. Why now? I had also been to support groups in the past. However, despite all the efforts I was making to find wellness and peace, my journey toward wholeness seemed to be derailed by a huge mountain called "mother-wounds."

The betrayal (misbeliefs about me and misdeeds toward me) that I experienced from my mother, and other mothering figures from my past, were affecting me and my current relationships, including my healing from other past trauma. I heard whisperings of a still, small voice, "So many have betrayed you, stolen things from you—your childhood, your youth—but you've betrayed yourself most of all. The right thing is the hardest thing to do." I had to face it, name it; and I did.

I hopped on a fast track of self-reflection and self-discovery, which included questioning my birth story and my life's purpose. And I discovered something unexpected along the way that led me to the *mother-heart* of God. He cares about the orphaned heart. He is a father to the fatherless. And, as I discovered, God is also a mother to the motherless, literally and figuratively.

Many of us have experienced deep mother-wounds or know someone who has experienced such wounds. Ten perfect mothers let alone one cannot fill that hole—that deep place of hurt and wounded-ness was redeemed for me in my wanderings through this life and through the discovery of the mother-heart of God, not just in an imaginary, spiritual way, but through flesh-and-blood, redemptive relationships that God, like *my mother*, chose for me.

As I wrote my life's story, first for myself and then for others, I came to the awareness that I was vulnerable and defenseless from the emotional abuse and neglect that I experienced. There should have been someone bigger and stronger to protect me. The lament of my heart was real to me. Bad things happen. Parents fail. Mothers (and fathers) fail, but I had lived in this land of lament too long, and I decided it was time to write these pieces of my story down.

There is a level of credibility that comes from experience. I am not a theologian, psychologist, or counselor, nor is it my intent to feminize a higher power that I call God who regards both male and female as his image bearers. I wrote my story, not out of fear or victimhood, but to shift my mental narrative by getting in touch with my vulnerability and writing about the unjust things that happened to me. I am not a child anymore. I have separated myself from that childhood state and am working through the remnants of those things that defined my identity, that enslaved me.

This book is about when I realized these impacts on my life (my awakening moment) and how I overcame them.

Our traumas impact our lives, work, and play. They steal our health, our emotional, physical, spiritual, relational, and social connection to others, and they even take away our creativity. Writing about what is unjust in my story gives me freedom from the tentacles of those who kept me in the prison of my own mind for four decades. There is nothing faker than living this life, replaying the loop of childhood traumatic events of the past. Being trapped by incidents that no longer exist in the current moment (re-experiencing past traumas as if they are happening in the present), bogs us down in this life and tires our soul.

This book will also address the question of where Mom was in my life, how my search for her led me to God's maternal Heart *(He became my Mama-G)*, and my own personal resolution over this broken relationship. Even those ordinary faults of moms (and dads), the bitterness, and, at times, the rage that it brings needs to be released. It does not depend on the magnitude of our individual stories, for this is not a competition. The wounds may not cause physical death, but they can be enough to cause emotional and spiritual scars.

Without real stories from my life, I cannot bring forth fully the emotions, the thoughts, and the beliefs that I battled for four decades. This book will take you into the deepest valleys of some of my greatest pain. I will move chapter by chapter into the valley, not out of selfishness but out of self-compassion. Just as God speaks against the sins visited upon His people, we, too, must name and confess the wrongs against us.

These traumas looked me in the eye and scared me away for a long time. As I battled with writing my story, I took back ground that allowed me to be authentic and vulnerable, dropping the different facades that haven't worked for me for four decades of my life. I don't want to live the rest of my life in the status quo. I want to live a life of wholeness and healing—leaning into the serendipitous moments of grace that I'm afforded every day of my life. Hope and healing are real. My experiences shared throughout this book will testify to that truth.

INTRODUCTION

Not by chance or happenstance, but by way of everything that has added up to this very moment of who I am, I can choose authenticity—an Esther moment—or I can hide behind the veil of past experiences, good or bad. I choose to drop the perfect. I choose to be real and authentic as I share my story. For you!

Note from the Author

This was an extremely difficult book to write, as you can imagine. I debated for a very long time on how much to write—how to write my story in order to help you understand how I felt as a child. As a reader, you will not find this book linear in a traditional storytelling style. As best as I can remember, I have written down my memories of the abuse of my childhood and onward, which resurfaced in my adolescence and young adulthood. I have also described how those events impacted me, even in my adult life.

A lot of times, my memory of childhood trauma was triggered when my own children were the ages I was when I went through my wounding. The processing of events occurred across different timeframes in my life. The stories might appear to be circling back and forth from childhood to adulthood, and at times may seem a little disjointed, with gaps in the storyline because as an adult I had to go back into my childhood and process events, which included working with therapists, mentors, recovery groups, and other women. Sometimes, I would move forward ten steps. At other times, I took twenty steps back. But I promise that in the end, I will show you my way out.

Are you wondering how I came out of my valley? It wasn't a sprint or even a marathon. I felt more like a snail who found its way across the patio, processing emotions sluggishly, sometimes feeling eternally stuck in those emotions with no light at the end of the tunnel and no end in sight on the journey. I couldn't scurry away, and I sometimes withdrew into my shell in fear. Then I would come out *fully* seen, yet cautiously trudging across the dry, scorching cement. At times, I circled back around to where I began, repeating the crazy journey over and over. I found myself in the repetition of the same patterns, a trajectory — a vortex. But as I journeyed, I left behind a trail of slime, the evidence of my journey. That is how you know I made it to the other side. Welcome to my slimy trail.

I don't claim that I'm completely healed, because I will always battle triggers and trust issues, but I have learned to cope with them. I have written and organized this book by themes that were downloaded to my soul by the very One who created me. I wrote these pieces of my story down by divine inspiration.

How to read this book:

This book is organized into five parts. At the end of each chapter, in Parts 1-4, I have offered some questions for your *Reflection*. I have also provided *Words of Encouragement* that you can walk away within the moment. I bring to the table all the aspects of how I processed my life and emotions. I bring to you the power of a *raw* story and authentic processing. I haven't held back;

my professional training and experiences; my understanding of brain science; the development of cognition, emotion, speech, language, and hearing; and my faith journey—these have all been reflected in this themed-memoir style of writing.

I pray these offer you *Hope*, which I discovered through my journey of facing my own wounds. I want to show you through my life experiences and healing that there is no pain too deep, no one too lost, nor is it ever too late to pick up the pieces of your past life and rebuild a new life with resiliency. I have written about my deep and personal stories from *Broken* to *Restored* and living into the serendipitous moments of God's grace. I have written these stories to give a voice to those with similar stories and to pass the gift of my healing forward.

In **Part 1, Purpose Stolen**, I deal with and take you into my childhood valley where I will show you how my purpose was stolen. In this section, I have chosen not to run away like a victim or a drama junkie but to put words and emotions to my stories.

In **Part 2, Created on Purpose**, I have processed and written down my realizations of my reality, glimpses of early mother-child bonding, what it was meant to be like, yet how I felt the contrary. Ultimately, I realized that no matter what, I was created by God's design for a specific purpose in this life.

In **Part 3, Broken Identity**, I will take you deeper into the valley of shadows, showing you how my early traumas impacted my adolescent and adult life.

In **Part 4, The Mother-Heart of God**, I will show you how the despair of my mother-wounds met the mother-heart of God—*the One* who spoke into and filled the mother void and dry places

15

of my soul.

In **Part 5, The Conclusion—My Decision**, I will show you my personal resolution over a dysfunctional mother-child relationship.

The reality is that it has been very difficult to share my deepest, darkest pain when my story exposes intergenerational trauma that has come down my family line. I battled with the thought that I was betraying the people who were supposed to love, nurture, protect, and comfort me. But as I wrote, and then re-read what I wrote, it helped me come to terms with what I endured— it was abuse, emotional abuse at its core. I realized that I was wasting a lot of years in denial that those who were supposed to love me could hurt me. I was feeling guilty for something I wasn't responsible for. This was the reason for my chaos, my social anxiety, and my extreme withdrawal from people, including the safe and loving people in my life. I even carried this relational brokenness into my marriage and into parenting my own children as you will read in this book.

It is my hope that by sharing my story, others will be inspired to share theirs.

If any of these events *trigger* you, I implore you to seek help from a trusted friend, pastor, or professional counselor and do whatever it takes to heal without minimizing your story or letting your offenders do the same.

This book, *Picking Up The Shards: Healing the Pain of Mother-Wounds, Discovering the Mother-heart of God*, is book one of the Broken to Restored series. The names of people in this book and locations have been changed to respect privacy and protect identities. If anyone recognizes themselves in this book and you are part of or have contributed to the traumas in my life, *I have forgiven you*. I admit it is an ongoing process and will be until we see the face of the One who will create a new heaven and a new earth where there will be no more pain, tears, or suffering.

PART I:

⁓

PURPOSE STOLEN

Introduction to Part I

E very person is created with Purpose for Destiny. As a young child, I remember wondering what it would be like when I grew up. Those years passed by quickly. And now, looking back, I can't help but feel that so much of my life was stolen — the innocence of childhood, sheer joy, happiness, playfulness, creativity, my dreams of a future and even my voice. Instead, it was replaced with fear, sadness, loss, and loneliness.

I had a deep void in my relationship with my mother and other maternal figures. The very person(s) I loved or I thought loved me deeply failed me in their connection to my soul, emotions, and spirit. The wounds I experienced as a child, whether they were wounds arising from what I didn't receive or wounds as a result of sin committed against me, disrupted my core, my creativity, my joy, and my purpose. These were betrayal wounds. My dreams were stolen and arrested by past trauma. This section in the book walks you through those early years.

Chapter 1

❧

FEARFULLY AND WONDERFULLY MADE

"The way we talk to our children becomes their inner voice."

—Peggy O' Mara

From my early years all the way into adulthood, I battled some emotional giants—rejection, abandonment, feelings of unworthiness, and the difficulty to embrace attention or delight from others. I felt I wasn't worthy of living my own life—the very life that God breathed into me. These years slipped away quickly, stolen from me as a result of my life's early traumas. In this chapter, I will walk you through these thoughts and emotions and how the tentacles of each wrapped their way through my brain.

❧

It was September of 1981. My parents had informed me of our plans to visit their homeland, India. I squealed with delight! In my two-and-half-year-old mind, going to India meant going to see my paternal grandparents—George and Sara—in their small village town. My mother was pregnant with my brother, and she planned on delivering the baby in her hometown, as she would have more support from her family than she would in Ghana, where we resided.

Before this visit to my grandparents' home, all I knew was my life with my parents in Ghana. While they worked at a local school as teachers, I was placed in the care of a woman I called Aunty Anna. She was a sweet lady. The only friend I had at the time was Milton. He was a five-year-old boy who lived next door. He was half British and half East Asian. Aunty Anna watched both of us at our home. Milton's parents were divorced, and his father was hardly ever home. I was happy to have Milton over all the time. He essentially became my older brother and best friend.

The only toy I owned was an old sponge doll. If I wasn't playing with Milton, I was playing with my doll. She had black hair, and her dress was made of brightly colored pink sponge. Mom always told me that I should take care of my doll and that it would be my only toy since that's all they could afford. Dollie was my treasure.

I didn't know why I felt as sad as Milton, but I did. Pictures of myself from that time period reveal a sorrowful little face, often marked with dried streams of tears. Milton was in several pictures with me. He, too, looked sad. Little did I know at the time, that he was hurting and broken because his mom had left him and his dad was never home. I empathized with Milton's lonely existence and kept him company until his dad picked him up late at night. My parents were at work for long hours, teaching and grading papers.

Milton and I were prevented from going outside to play. The perimeter of the school ground was surrounded by thick guinea grass, short trees, and shrubs native to this part of West Africa. The grass was burnt down multiple times during the year. This is how the ground was cleared for cultivation, which also meant snakes found new homes in yards and garages of the houses on campus, including ours! Aunty Anna told us that it was too dangerous to play there because of the snakes writhing on and scorpions scrambling over the dirt road in front of our home, which led to the school grounds where my parents worked. The dangers lurking outside—puff adders, green mambas, cobras, and pythons were no invitation to us. We enjoyed each other's company along with Aunty Anna.

One day, Milton and I made a trip to the school with Aunty Anna. A large crowd had gathered on a balcony looking down at the scene below. A goat tied to a tree trunk had been killed by a python. People were quietly waiting to get a glimpse of the giant serpent that would eventually come back in stealth for its prey. And, indeed, the python returned. I couldn't believe my eyes or understand the sight before me! How could a snake swallow up a whole animal?

Another time, I remember my parents going outside our home with a lantern at night because the chickens sounded distressed in their coop. My father, with his 5′6″ frame, bare muscular hands, and determined square face was soon facing a king cobra with its hood spread out, ready for attack. Daddy, being an outrageously courageous man, took after the snake.

Mother pleaded for him not to confront it. My father eventually backed away, as he was no match for the giant serpent. Later, my parents would retell a story about an eight-foot-long snake.

Needless to say, there were snakes literally everywhere so Milton and I spent a lot of time indoors with our loving caregiver. Aunty Anna married shortly after these events. Thus, after only being with me a short time, my first caregiver moved away.

∽

My next memories were of visiting and staying with my playful Grandpa George and my very nurturing Grandma Sara in India. They lived in a 1500-square-foot home surrounded by coconut groves and teak and cocoa trees. The minute we arrived at my grandparents' home, my curious little self followed them around everywhere. The smell of the ground as the first showers of the North East monsoon rains arrived, the crushed rocks under my bare feet, and experiencing the wet mud on my fingers—it was all exhilarating.

My grandparents were thrilled to have me visit—a fine opportunity to spoil their first and only grandchild at the time (a child they were meeting in person for the very first time). I was intrigued by the stories of their life in the village—the sights and sounds, the cows in the stall, the chickens in their coop, and the goats in the yard. There was a lot to see and explore in this small town.

Although their living circumstances were poor, it didn't matter to me, as I had so much fun. I spent time pulling the hay from the haystack and feeding the cows. The most thrilling adventure was gathering eggs from the living room and front patio seat cushions where chickens sneaked in to lay their eggs. I carefully collected those eggs as if I had discovered little pots of gold. Grandpa used his harvesting knife curved like a hook and tied to a pole to pick ripe guavas, mangoes, and cashew fruit to provide me an instant snack.

I was always ready to dance and sing for them. To my grandparents' delight, I made up stories with lively characters using my then very English accent that I acquired during my time in Africa hanging out with Milton.

They were enamored with my charming and entertaining personality, even capturing my stories and singing on cassette tapes. I remember my grandma saying, "What an amazing three-year-old child. She is smart, carefree, and full of life."

At that age, I was fascinated by hats and shoes. Every dress had to be worn with a hat and a matching pair of shoes. I can't imagine that I had that many clothes, but whatever I had I wore proudly and well.

Grandpa walked me to the local nursery school that was tucked behind a local provision store down the street from their home. Boy, did I love it there! I was eager to get dressed every morning for school. I skipped and hopped along the way, holding grandpa's pinky finger as I chattered away and hopscotched between the puddles and the loose mud in the street during our walks to pre-school.

My life took a turn when Mom decided she was going to her parents' house, as her due date was fast approaching. We stayed a few weeks longer at my paternal grandparents' home until my mom gave birth to my brother. Mother recalled that I wasn't very excited by his arrival. He wasn't a doll that I could play with. I begged for him to be sent back to his home! Dollie was my constant and preferred companion. We went to my maternal grandparents' home shortly thereafter.

Although I was secretly heartbroken to leave my paternal grandparents' home, I was excited and eager to visit and get to know my maternal grandparents. They lived in a large home on an acreage surrounded by cocoa and rubber plantations. Grandpa was gone most of the day to tend to his livestock and his cultivation. Mother's younger siblings still lived at home. I instantly connected with one of my uncles who was still single. I didn't feel that lonely because he kept me company. My young uncle fed me, bathed me, and essentially turned into my care-giver as my mom was busy focusing on my newborn brother. We stayed at my mother's house for several months, and I began to wonder about my own birth story.

What was my birth story? I knew I was born in Ghana, Africa. Mom had always talked about her difficult pregnancy. She said that I was born in a hospital with a crowd of young medical students watching, and they were smitten by me—a beautiful, bald-headed, Indian baby girl.

In contrast, she would also share these words about my birth story:

"When you were born, you looked so beautiful. Your skin was so soft and fair, and you looked just like my sister, Sissy. Then, about three days after your birth, black spots appeared around your fingernails that spread up your fingers. Within a couple of weeks, your skin became dark. Your head was completely bald." Mother also told me that when my grandmother, Sara, received the news of my birth, she cried because I was the first grandchild and a girl (not a boy) with very dark-complexioned skin (not light) and no hair—she wept with sadness. (Interestingly, I personally never heard those words from my grandmother.)

The very first time I heard this story, my heart sank. I could hear my mother's disappointment—her broken expectations. Culturally, a female child was not valued. And, if you were an extremely dark-skinned, bald-headed girl, it was even worse—it was a curse. Everything about me, including my physical characteristics, earned me the title (and prejudice) of a "less than" child. And it spiraled downhill from there.

This became the mantra of the maternal side of my family. I remember going to family gatherings, holidays, weddings, and funerals, where every single time, without fail, I was labeled as the dark-colored granddaughter of my grandpa Papi from this self-proclaimed reputable family in town. I continued to hear how dark my skin was over and over. It felt, even at the young age of three, as if there was a quest afoot to determine who was the fairest in the land, or maybe of the clan. Because of this strongly held mantra, I quickly withdrew socially. I felt isolated and developed social anxiety.

As a child, people labeled me as withdrawn, shut down, and wordless—I was frequently asked if I had "swallowed a banana." I was often taunted about the way I conversed: "Do you have a tongue in your mouth? Wait, we can't see your tongue. You must have swallowed it!"

Over time, these voices from my maternal nurturing figures played like messages on tape, repeating over and over again. As these labels rang strongly through my head, the first lie I began to believe was that I was born beautiful and quickly turned ugly (dark). In my mind's eye, beautiful and dark could not coexist. My ugly parts defined me. I began to see myself through the lens of my mother and her sisters, whom I felt did not value me for who I was.

This idea continued to play out even later in life. One hot, summer afternoon, my brother and I, along with our mother, visited one of my aunts. Before I even stepped into her home, her square face with quizzical eyes and a frown stuck to her forehead looked me up and down from the top of my head to the bottom of my toes with great concern. "What was she about to say," I wondered, after this very lengthy assessment. Finally, I heard the words dart straight in my face, "I wonder who would want to marry you?"

All through my childhood and well into adulthood I continued to believe this lie that I was the dark, ugly duckling of the family who wouldn't amount to much. I didn't have a future, and no man would ever want to marry me. This core message defined me—I strongly believed that my dark color determined my destiny.

There was always discussion among my aunts about my color choices of clothing. They determined what made me look darker or lighter. These women in my life–my mothering figures–determined what I thought of as pleasing.

Womanhood, as modeled through the paternal side of my family, was vastly different. Despite my mother's claim that my birth was a disappointment to my paternal grandmother, Sara, she was my saving grace. A woman of incredible strength, knowledge of the trends of times, world history, and local happenings; she was a guru. Grandma Sara was a nurturing soul—a loving person of class and character. She filled the gap for me when my parents were absent and fulfilled the parental role of mother and father for a good part of my life, for which I am forever grateful.

⟳

Fast forward twenty-five years, I remember standing at the threshold of marriage—the day had finally arrived. A day that people told me, and that I believed, would never come—culturally, and according to my family, I was an old hag! I was dressed in a beautiful Indian outfit that looked like a ball gown. After twenty-eight years, the dreams I had as a little girl were finally coming to pass.

As I reflected back during that eve of my marriage, I thought of the arranged marriage proposals that were commonplace in India. A suitor's family would meet the prospective bride in a social context or at her home. When I was twenty-one, I had completed both a bachelor's and a master's degree from a premier Institute in India. I had just arrived at my Grandma Sara's home after graduate school—exhausted, yet relieved to have completed my college education. As I was resting, a man seeking a marriage alliance for his son came to our porch and inquired about me. I passed the educational criteria with flying colors, like a whiz! However, he gave me the ultimate look of judgment, spat on the ground with great disgust, and said "This... uhh... this... is the girl? Oh, no way! My son isn't going to marry this girl." I couldn't believe this man had come into my grandma's house and belittled me.

After several marriage proposals, and several men, I finally met the one that I wanted to marry. Ironically, this one was quasi-arranged. A cousin of mine knew a friend of my future husband's and had given him a photograph of me. Tom, my husband's friend, never responded. A couple of years later, I received a call from a lady I had never met. According to her, she was hosting Tom (the friend who never called) during a conference he was attending in the same town. "Umm, we think we found you a guy! I have seen your picture, but you haven't seen his, right? He is about 4 feet tall."

I wondered who this random woman was. How did she feel so confident that she could set me up with "a guy?" I instantly and politely declined her offer. She tried to convince me that if her daughter was of age, she would consider giving her in marriage to him.

Oh, no, no, no! This is not happening. *I quickly felt compelled to call my close friend who said, "Girl, this is from God. Just start praying for your wedding details." She then added, "You might want to start finding a wedding dress!" Oh dear, now I had to add my friend to the list of folks who had utterly lost their minds. I shut down the idea, thanked her for being a good but "crazy" friend, and went on about my life.*

It was quiet for a while, until one evening six months later, I happened to visit a family with some friends of mine. They were having a mini get together followed by "prayer time." Someone came up to me and said, "In ninety-nine days from today, you will meet your husband!"

I have to flee this place, *I thought. Prayers and prophecies?!? I sneaked out and drove home, secretly wishing and asking God, "What if the prophecy comes true?" I started marking my calendar, putting an "X" mark on each* *day that passed. (Yes, you are welcome to laugh out loud). Day ninety-nine arrived and nothing! I knew I was right! That whole thing—the prayer, the prophet, the prophecy... a bunch of lies, at least that is what I concluded. That night, I came back from work and turned on the television, vegged out on the couch, totally disappointed at God. I made a decision—that I would stay single and* **choose** *to be happy for the rest of my life.*

Before the end of that night (the ninety-ninth day), however, my future husband indeed picked up the phone and called me! Unbeknownst to me, Tom had given my phone number to him! I was terrified, yet elated. I couldn't have made this stuff up in my head. God was at work bringing my spouse to me.

After a few months of courtship, we were engaged. The wedding was set and we were soon to be married in the United States. Someone finally chose me **completely** *and* **totally** *for who I was.*

Most of my mother's family resided in North America by the time my marriage took place. And so there we were—together—practicing all the details the night before the big event. I was excited and giddy all at the same time thinking about our big day. At one point, we were practicing walking down the aisle, and just as the music began playing, my Aunt Sissy spotted me, ran over, and said, "How are *you* this pretty? I cannot believe this! How could this be *you*?" My soon-to-be husband responded to this brash comment, replying to my aunt, "You have known her for all these years, and now is when you realize she is beautiful?"

My husband frequently quoted Psalm 139 over me. "You are fearfully and wonderfully made." He consistently affirmed me with this verse from the very first day we met. Yet I still battled the thought, *What on earth does this man know about me, that he calls me beautiful on the inside and out?* I simply couldn't accept the fact that someone delighted in me. All my life, I had heard nothing but voices of judgment. The tapes that had played in my head on repeat for almost three decades still haunted me. I was a veteran of self-talk sabotage: ugly, invaluable, unwanted, dark and black, unworthy of a future, and unworthy of marriage. The power of those words—that broken recording—played on in my life. I continued to believe that my color determined my destiny.

After we were married, we moved into our first home, which was 1700 square feet. There wasn't a lot of room for me to hide from my husband in that house. The best I could do was to hide my tiny frame inside extra-large T-shirts and baggy jeans. After my wanderings around North America, I moved in with my husband with all of my belongings, which fit in a suitcase and a handful of boxes. The finest of my clothing belonged to Goodwill. Once we were settled, my husband graciously and kindly shopped with me, where I got a much-needed wardrobe makeover (with clothes that were actually my size). All I could see was my dark, ugly, invaluable self—unworthy of my husband's attention or God's delight.

The phrase "fearfully and wonderfully" made absolutely no sense to me. This was the last thing I wanted to hear from my husband.

I had a difficult time receiving words of affirmation, affection, or compliments from anyone.

Within the first three years of marriage, we had to move again. I was pregnant with our first child and had been placed on total bed rest from complications I had developed during my pregnancy. With pregnancy hormones raging and my anxiety at an all-time high, my mind pranced around with fear, hitting the proverbial roof. I lived paralyzed at the thought of being alone while at the same time trying to flee (with what felt like an elephant in my belly, which happened to be my unborn child). I was paranoid by the sound of the second hand of the clock ticking in my living room.

I had frequent dreams about this despicable, evil man breaking in and chasing after me. I surely passed tons of cortisol and other stress-related hormones into my daughter's bloodstream. The silence was worse than the debilitating, physical pain I was experiencing and the impending fear that lurked all around me. Paranoia chased me around my own home like a monster with giant claws. My brain was constantly on high alert. I literally felt trapped by fear in my own house and in my own body, unable to move or do much. I was on bed rest for bleeding and a myriad of other complications, including the risk of preterm labor. I worked from home, lying in bed well into my third trimester. I was unable to keep much down and was miserable, and I thought to myself that maybe I was replicating my mother's difficult pregnancy. We had to move away from our first home again due to my husband finding a new job in another town. This would be my twenty-third move in my lifetime.

The dysfunction and isolation I had experienced all my life were suddenly screaming in my face. I thought perhaps this was the life I deserved. My inner critical voice stated with crystal clear clarity, "You are making a big deal out of nothing."

None of these circumstances or my emotions were that bad after all. Some friends and family members shared words of sympathy, others passed judgment and condemnation on my new situation with my pregnancy. I felt that neither my story nor I mattered. I was convinced that I was somehow responsible—God was punishing me for some unpardonable sin from my past life.

Life all around began to look like a mistake. I was having a pity party with myself. Indeed, now God had made an even bigger mistake! I began to feel like a prisoner of my own life in my own home. God had removed me from two other continents, and now I was on a third, with loneliness and isolation as my two best friends.

Questioning my whole existence was nothing new. I had questioned my purpose many times, since I was a young teen, in fact. And now, as an adult, I had arrived here one more time. I continued to question my reality, my existence, and God. What was I to do with my nomadic life? I was married, pregnant, living in our first home together as a couple, and yet, that small semblance of normalcy I had experienced at Grandma Sara's felt like a disappearing wisp.

I silently battled and argued with God. I questioned if He was really and truly with me all my life—with his "abiding presence." I asked him if he was real and why he bothered creating me? I was convinced that God must have made a mistake and it would have been better if he hadn't created me.

In my depressed state, I began crying out to him, "God, are you out there somewhere? Are you in my world? My world feels bloody lonely right now." In case he was out there somewhere in the Universe floating around on some cloud, either he didn't have time for me or he was busy helping someone else. I recounted my first experiences of God and faith, trying to believe he was still around. I felt totally abandoned by Him at this moment.

When I read Psalm 139:5-6 (NIV), "You hem me in behind and before, and you lay your hand upon me. Such knowledge is too wonderful for me, too lofty for me to attain." These verses were the biggest lie I had ever heard. I was mad at the God of the Universe for creating me. What a liar I thought He was!

∽

Reflection Questions

Was there a time in your life when you were judged for who you were, for the way you looked, spoke, behaved, or for just **being you***?*

Have you felt unwanted or rejected simply for existing in this world? Have you dealt with a lack of acceptance from your family, extended family—biological, fostered, adopted, or any significant caregiver or attachment figure in your life?

What were the core family messages you heard? Can you identify with one core message you have repeatedly heard growing up? How did that impact you?

Has anyone told you (like they told me), that you wouldn't amount to anything or you wouldn't have a future because of who you really are?

Have you felt unworthy of delight and attention from some-one who genuinely cared about you just like I did with my husband? Have you found it difficult to embrace the thought of God delighting in you?

〜

Words of encouragement

If you answered "Yes" to any of the questions above, can I burst your bubble and tell you that you are human!

You are not alone!

We were created by God with emotions, and our childhood experiences and significant attachment figures do shape our inner messages.

Some of these messages were what was spoken to us and maybe some of these messages were perceived because they weren't what we needed to hear. Words have power; both words others speak to you and words you speak to yourself. You can subconsciously sabotage yourself through the words you choose to speak to yourself.

We heal when we face the reality of what shaped us, even if we don't have control over the situations or circumstances that led us to this point in our existence. We also need to feel those deep-set emotions. They are real.

∽

Final Note

There is hope for healing, and we can come out on the other side when we commit, by choice, to a path and process of healing of our inner core. I questioned God about his existence and why he created me. I even challenged him—I told God that if he existed, he could wear his big boy underpants if he wanted to deal with me. He can perfectly deal with our emotions and our "just as we are" selves. We have permission to feel and talk to ourselves, to others, and to someone bigger and higher than us—God. We should be free to express ourselves, asking God to answer our questions and to show up in tangible ways—in ways that we can comprehend and feel.

Chapter 2

⌒

WHERE IS HOME
AND WHERE IS MOM?

"Home is a place I yearn to be;
it is still in the making."

—Anita M. Oommen

H ere we will address the question, "Where was Mom in my life?" This chapter will take you through my struggles with my mother-child relationship, the stolen bond and broken attachment relationship that occurred, and the woundedness from that broken bond that I carried into my adult years and into my parenting. My search for Mom ultimately led me to question God.

⌒

African by birth, and Indian by origin, I spent my younger years between two continents. During the course of my nomadic wanderings, I spent a good decade living mostly with my dad's family, sometimes with my mom's family, and occasionally with other temporary families, guardians, boarding schools, and hostels with terrorizing wardens, matrons, and everything in between! I felt like a vagabond, moving from place to place and losing a sense of security in the families I had lived with. Now, as an adult and a new mother at home with my own baby, thousands of miles away on a third continent, I was triggered with memories of my own childhood.

Where was home? I wondered if something was wrong with me? I began to question where my mom was when I was a young child? Was she really present?

I had come to grips with my birth story, but why was I questioning my purpose well into the third and fourth decades of my life? I had many people involved in my life's journey, however, my heart felt terribly *orphaned*.

There was a sting in my heart that ran through the deepest depths of my soul—an utter sense of dejection and abandonment that I just couldn't put my finger on or wrap my head around.

Now a mother myself, as I held my own baby girl, I wondered what she was going to be like—what talents and gifts and personality she would embody. Was she going to be like me as a young girl, ready to sing and dance and entertain the world? Or was she going to be like the other part of me, socially withdrawn, anxious, and lonely?

Why was I having flashbacks of my own childhood? Did having my own child trigger my young, inner child? I was transported back in time to my three-year-old self. I began recalling pieces of my life from that time period.

⟡

I was living with my mother's family around the time my brother was born. I had just celebrated my third birthday at the home of my maternal grandparents, Pappi and Eli. It was my aunt's wedding (my dad's only sister), and Mom was in a frenzy due to running terribly behind schedule. We had to leave shortly to take a taxi to my paternal grandparents' house for pre-wedding festivities.

I was excited to wear a hat to my aunt's wedding, but Mother decided it was too hot and out of place for me to wear a hat to a wedding in the local culture. So she decided she was going to tie a ribbon in my hair. I should give her credit for finding one that matched my dress. I didn't dare move my head or flinch when she pulled the ringlets out of my tight curls, yanking my hair up in a half ponytail. *Ouch, that hurt.* I knew if she couldn't get the ribbon tied tight enough, or if I dared let out a whimper due to the pain, she would slap me across my face with the comb—across my three-year-old little cheeks—as a consequence

41

of my protest.

The harsh comb spankings were so hard that I cried in pain regardless of how much I tried to hold it in. I can still feel my red skin burning and stinging in pain. The more I cried, the tighter the ribbon was pulled, to the point that my head began to hurt. I detested the new hairstyle I was forced to embrace.

The more I cried, the more I flinched, and the torture continued. In addition to spankings with the comb, Mom would twist the skin on my arms until skin came off my upper arm. If I protested, she would take to twisting my ears, one time to the point that I thought my ears weren't hardy enough to stay on. "She is so stubborn," said one aunt. "She fights you to put a ribbon in her hair?" the comb slapping across my face once more. I was laughed and jeered at with sadistic pleasure, which radiated from the lines of the corners of their mouths as they broke into hysterical laughter in unison. Because of moments like this, I permanently lost my childhood smile.

One night after family prayer time, which was consistently practiced every night, I was put outside in the dark for some petty three-year-old mistake I had committed at 9:00 p.m. I remember Grandma Eli asking Mom if I wouldn't be terrified, but that did not deter her from placing me outside. Mother's voice echoed, "She is so stubborn. She deserves to stand right there, outside in the dark."

As I stood alone in the night, I was terrified. The world around me was dark and eerie. Bats flew across the rubber trees. The owl hooted at the night. I heard nocturnal animals, crickets, and the rustling of leaves. Could it be snakes? I remembered my mom's stories about the snakes in Africa. I had seen several, big and small. I determined something was coming to swallow me alive. My heart raced so fast that I could hear it pounding loudly in my chest and in my head. I felt alone, abandoned, and scared in the thick of the darkness. Street lights barely lit this small village town. I looked up into the dark sky to see if the moon would be my companion as the dark of night engulfed me.

I heard the women inside the house laughing and peering through the window to investigate how I was responding. Looking through the blur of my tear-filled eyes, I couldn't see much. I heard someone ask if I was crying. Then I heard these unflinching words, which cut me to the core, "What a *stubborn* child. Let her stand out there until she has learned a good lesson the hard way tonight."

The sadistic pleasure radiating through those windows made the darkness around me even darker. I stood up straight. I told myself that I would neither cry nor show these people that I had cried anymore. That night left a deep, dark mark on my young soul. I held it all in and sent the heavy emotions welling up inside of me somewhere inside a deep abyss in my heart. On the inside, I was standing tall, suppressing all my emotions. I learned it was safer to shut my emotions *in* to survive the agony of abandonment. I determined that they didn't like me. After all, I was dark-skinned, stubborn, and the ugly child of the family. Finally, after what seemed like an eternity, Mother came and got me. I wondered if these were some of the ways disciplining a child was modeled for Mom. Did she personally experience being disciplined in this manner?

I hated this environment. This certainly didn't feel like home. Yes, it takes a village to raise a child, but the problem was I had two different kinds of villages raising me. I developed a divided belief system within me, which I believed was *because of me.* My paternal side and my maternal side treated me very differently from one another. These time-warped messages through contradicting stories that I had heard over time left my young mind conflicted. The dichotomy ingrained in my brain was that I was highly valuable with great potential—acceptable to my father and his family with all my character flaws. On the other hand, I was dark, ugly, stubborn, and did not measure up or deserve much from my mother or her family.

Financially, things were tight for my parents, especially with a growing family and no work. It was time to leave for Nigeria and join my dad who had moved there from Ghana for a job. Honestly, I was happy to leave. We went back to my Grandpa George and Grandma Sara's home to say our goodbyes before heading to the airport to begin a new chapter in our lives.

Nigeria

Getting lost in Nairobi, Kenya was my next adventure!

My new brother, who was about six months old, was sick on our journey to Nigeria. Over the years, Mother recounted the story of how I was lost in an airport when we were in transit in Nairobi, Kenya. My mother had her hands full and I took off, according to her account. I was found on the tarmac getting on another aircraft. A crew member who had watched me bolt ran after me and walked me back into the building. As I entered the building, an Indian family heading to Nigeria identified me, as they knew my parents. The family kept me with them, and I had enough sense to tell them I was lost, giving them plenty of information. I remember feeling completely alone. Where was Mom? Would I find her again? Maybe this time it was my mischievous little self. Or was this a result of neglect or lack of supervision?

These stories were made into jokes and passed around the family my entire life, as I've heard them on repeat, over and over again.

⟡

Reflection Questions

Is there a time in your life when you were triggered by child-hood memories of your life, when your children were about the age that soul wounding occurred in your life?

Is there a time when you felt that home wasn't what it should have been because of what was done to you? Maybe you haven't experienced being pulled out into the yard or onto the porch, but have you felt or perceived parental neglect by sins of omission (e.g., not providing you with protection, love, and nurture)?

∽

Words of encouragement

You will unzip your wounding when you're ready. God has created our brains to be able to file away those traumatic childhood memories in a fragmented way, stored in the primitive part of our brain, in our hippocampus*, as a way to survive our everyday lives.[1] Trauma-based flashbacks are not pleasant; however, with the right help from a trained professional counselor, you can ease into the window of tolerance gently and slowly in order to process past childhood traumatic events.

You have great resilience to have survived.

Be kind to yourself and practice compassion.

Go into your past and process events slowly.

༄

Final Note

The Bible says the enemy comes like a thief in the night to steal, kill, and destroy! And he knows that he can steal our joy, peace, and mental sanity by wreaking havoc on our limbic system which contains the parts of our brain that processes emotions.[2] *However, with the right help from a trained professional counselor and spiritual resources (in my case, I considered the Holy Spirit my counselor) you can gently and slowly begin to process past childhood traumatic events.*

Chapter 3

~☺~

UNSEEN
AND FORGOTTEN?

*"If you can't go back to your mother's
womb, you'd better be a good fighter."*

—Anchee Min

*"We all come out of the womb needing love
in order to grow and develop properly."*

—Ken Poirot

I felt unseen and forgotten by my mom and others in my
life, and this seemed to be the theme of my early years. In
this chapter, I will walk you through my unseen and forgotten
world, where I was alone in my worst moments and developed
"isolating" and "shutting inward" as mechanisms for survival.
My dreams of playing in puddles and blowing dandelions were
stolen from me! I bring to light the loss of childhood playfulness
and innocence.

PICKING UP THE SHARDS

ᨳ

By the time we moved to Nigeria (where I thought I would truly and finally find home), a lot of my life was already displaced as we were constantly on the move. We lived inland in a small town in southwestern Nigeria. I picked up the local language, Yoruba. I fluently conversed in Yoruba and translated conversations between my neighbors and my parents. The hot, arid temperatures cracked the clay ground around our house. Water was scarce. When we had a few short days of uninterrupted water supply, my parents stored water in large drums in the garage. There were many times when my father had to drive out to our friends' homes in nearby towns and collect drinking water in barrels and gallon cans. Tsetse flies and mosquitoes seemed to survive these environments. They transmitted malaria around town. I frequently contracted malaria, in addition to UTIs.

Life, as I knew it to that point, had changed every few years. This set up my young and growing mind to experience instability and displacement that felt worse than my experiences of physical illnesses. As much as I had experienced a mother's physical care in living with her, she was not fully *emotionally* present. In my young mind, my mother never stood up for me. Under her watch, I was belittled, labeled, and abused, emotionally and verbally. She never fought for my personhood, my worth, dignity, or self-image. Seldom did I experience words of affirmations, positive feedback, or validation from her or others in her sphere of influence. I *only* felt intense abandonment and rejection. I was never good enough or wonderful enough to meet all of her expectations.

Perhaps Mother *didn't* know how to connect authentically. Could she have experienced early abandonment or neglect? Maybe there was common ground that we shared. Regardless of what the reasons were behind this, in my mind, I questioned where Mom was? I still question where she is? Is she loving me from a distance? Has she stopped loving me? Is her love conditional? Perhaps the river of her love was flowing upstream against resistance and withdrawal as I wasn't fulfilling the role of "scapegoat daughter" or "fantasy daughter."

Because of my brother's chronic respiratory illness when we were young, Mother spent a lot of energy worrying about him. She stayed up around the clock many nights, expending a lot of her mental, emotional, and physical energy to tend to him. This left her depleted, without much left to offer me besides her sleep-deprived, energy-deflated state. This did not help my mindset of feeling forgotten. Mom was always "kind and nice" to me when I was sick (e.g., when I had malaria or severe kidney infections, which I frequently experienced, requiring me to be hospitalized). But otherwise, in my four-year-old mind, I felt that she didn't care for me as much. What I did not understand then is that she needed to feel wanted.

"Your brother is too sick, and I hope we can keep him alive until the morning," said Mother. The trauma of that day left a lasting impact on me. That evening, she told me that the next day they were going to a distant town with my brother to see a doctor, and it would be a twelve-hour journey. She informed me that I needed to stay behind. I didn't realize, however, that I would be staying by myself at home with food and water set out on the dining room table. As my parents tended to my brother through the night, preparing for their journey, I sat wondering which would come sooner: the morning sun breaking through the horizon or the news that my brother was no longer alive. I was despondent, to say the least. Dad didn't say much. He tore a strip of cotton fabric off an old pillow cover and rolled it up to make a spout long enough to dip in a bowl of water that resided on the bedside table. In the absence of an IV, this served as an innovative contraption to keep my brother hydrated. My brother sucked on that piece of wet, rolled up fabric and stayed alive.

I barely slept that night as I watched for the first signs of daybreak through a huge, drape-less window—pink streaks painting the sky and the familiar smell of coffee—wondering what was to come. As the morning sun arose, I quickly ran to check on my brother who was gasping for air, gurgles and hoarseness emanating from his chest as he struggled to stay alive. These were not the regular cries that I was accustomed to. I certainly did not want my little brother, my only companion, to die.

My parents left, with the doors locked, and handed the house keys to a neighbor, Ms. Ella, who was asked to check on me after work. My little mind could not understand *why* I was left behind. I cried the entire time I was left alone in that locked house. I remember running around the house, jumping up in the air as high as my legs would take me to reach and bang the door handle which was too high. I tried everything I knew to open the door, to no avail.

I finally gave up and resorted to waiting until dark for my parents and my sick brother, my only buddy, to return home— hopefully, alive. My food and water stayed untouched. I finally heard the keys click in the door as my parents returned home late that night. As the door clicked open, my racing heart and my splitting head finally came to a halt. The freeze-flight-fight loop had drained me. I was more relieved than angry, nonetheless bitter toward Mother when these words rolled off her tongue, "We couldn't see the doctor because he was out of town!"

This was a pattern that was repeated throughout my early childhood. My brother would get terribly sick, and my mother would worry about trying to keep him alive. Through this cycle, I internalized the message that keeping my brother alive was important, but that I was fine and forgotten!

Where was my father in all this, you might be wondering? Outside of work, Daddy retreated to his own world, mostly reading and listening to the BBC news and classical music station on his handheld radio. My father did instill in us the love of reading. His books lined every inch of our home—in stacks on the floor, in the corner of a room, on every table, and our only bookcase that was overflowing. Both my brother and I were reading the British Ladybird series before we could even hold a pencil. My father was exceedingly proud when he heard us read words from his adult fiction books. He frequently gave us special-ordered, leather-bound English classics. But my escape of curling up with books and reading was short lived. The calm I experienced in my world of books was broken too easily by the chaos around me.

From my earliest memories, there was marital discord in our home, constantly on display and never saved for later. My parents' love language was "arguing." Mother religiously took us to a local Baptist church. But Dad stayed home due to their war over religion, which was among the many things in life they were conflicted about, including family, finances, and even illness. Right after their escalated episodes, I felt I had to hide for safety. Sometimes, in a fit of anger, Dad would throw a book or anything he found across the room. Then, Mom would scream at us! I would sit with my brother in the corner of the room until the storm overhead passed.

If we were to open our mouths, even accidentally, then spankings, verbal barrage, or both would be directed at us. I would get on my knees with my palms up together above my head (with my brother tucked directly behind me) and beg Mom not to beat me as she aimed her verbal barrage toward me. I wondered somehow if I had done something wrong or contributed in some way to the fights and discord in the family.

Despite the marital discord, my daddy *never* told me I was dumb. In my mind, Dad was the only one who actually "valued me." He was a man of very few words. If he said anything to me, much of what he said was affirming and of value, and I would store it in my heart, although I didn't feel remotely *at home*. My dad was protective of me and even told me I was exceptionally smart and *special* because of my left-handedness. Culturally, the custom was to change left-handedness because it was considered less than, a strange phenomenon, ominous, and had a great stigma attached—ultimately it was shameful. My father assured me that no one would ever be allowed to spank my left hand or beat me into changing my handedness. If there was anything I was proud of, it was indeed my left-handedness. I boldly showed off to everyone how "beautifully" I wrote using my left hand!

On some weekends, my parents met with family friends. As far as I can remember, their children were older than I was, either older teens or young adults. As the youngest member at small gatherings or big parties, I tried to participate as best I could. One evening, we were at Uncle Pete's house. There were music and dancing coming from an upstairs room. The grownups

54

were having a good time downstairs with conversation, food, and drink, so I followed the sounds of the music and drums upstairs. I knocked on the door to the room only to find it locked. I strained my ears first against the door and then against the wall to listen to the fun happening inside. I ended up falling asleep at the foot of the door, which was at the top of the stairs. I remember hearing my own piercing screams as I landed with a loud thud at the foot of the deep stairwell. Within seconds, I had an audience of adults in the house sprinting for the stairway—I survived, albeit traumatized.

My four-year-old school life was also traumatic. I was sent to grade one to start school as there was no kindergarten, and I was the youngest in the class. Every single day a boy would steal my sandwich. The first time it happened, I came home and told my mom and she just laughed, thinking it was a joke. Day after day, week after week, my sandwich was taken. One day, everything within me finally welled up, and I had no choice but to defend myself. I took a broomstick that I found at the corner of the classroom and I beat the boy up when he attempted to take my sandwich. He never touched my sandwich for the rest of the year.

I went to the local public school for three years. Every single morning, I cried until I had no more tears. I begged my parents, especially Mom, not to send me back to school one more day. I knew what awaited me—punishment, corporal and other forms, was the norm. Wooden chairs were hurled at me. My arms and legs were hit with a cane. The worst was when the teacher would call me out and I would have to stand in front of the class. When this happened, I had to bend forward, wrap my arm under the back of my thigh and then pull my hand to my face, putting one finger in my mouth, and then stand there on one leg for what seemed like hours. This lasted until my head hurt and every muscle in my body was strained. In my misery, I felt forgotten, not just by Mom, but also by the world. When I went home and told my parents about school, Mom's response was that school was where I needed to be to get an "education."

One afternoon, I escaped from my classroom, walking off the school premises and following the dirt road. I knew this road, as it bordered the Baptist church. I followed the dirt road to a T-intersection. I had to cross the main road, which was quite busy. I looked both ways, closed my eyes, and ran across the road with my heart thumping, my head hot and my face flushed. I had to do this before someone found out. I ran as fast as I could, weaving on the dirt road that wrapped around homes. To my relief, I found my house. I had successfully escaped hell only to realize I was trying to open a locked door. I sat out in the midday sun, roasting at what felt like a thousand degrees.

When my parents returned home that evening, they found me dehydrated and close to collapsing from the brutal exposure to the sun. I received a full-blown dose of verbal shelling. In their fury, my parents decided that a family friend who taught at the Baptist school would keep an "eye" on me. Dare I risk my safety again, Mom told me that I would get in trouble, deep trouble. I took Mom's words seriously, but my survival instincts kicked in and led me out to the dirt road again. When I saw my parents' friend threatening me, however, I went back to the prison-like school and back to class only to find the teacher waiting with her verbal abuse and corporal punishment. I soon developed a phobia of authority figures.

I felt helpless and hopeless, unable to defend myself. The hairs on the nape of my neck still stand up when I think about how I cried those unending tears every morning. Friday nights brought me some relief, as I didn't have to go to school for two days. Sunday nights, however, brought on fits of fear and anxiety as I sobbed my lungs out. Would someone ever rescue me? Maybe one day?

There were tiny bright spots in my early childhood in Nigeria.

Occasionally, on the weekends when my brother wasn't sick, we would go visit my father's cousins who also lived and worked as teachers in a different state. My favorite weekends were when we visited my three loud and playful cousins (all boys). My cousins, my brother, and I played pillow fights, sprayed water on each other from the garden hose, and biked around the school campus. We turned rambunctious when we were together—unleashed. No one came screaming after us, so we played to our hearts' content. My uncle and aunt were like my second parents. They knew me and my brother from the time we were infants from our days in Ghana, and I felt at *home* when we visited them. Although these visits were short-lived, their house was my second home. When Sunday came around, I was always sad to leave. Every time. To date, my uncle and aunt and my three cousins are like parents and siblings to me. (After I started writing this book, my uncle passed away. I lost a precious dad and father figure.)

One day, the torture of school finally came to an end. My mother decided to take me out and sent me and my brother to a neighbor who was not working at the time. My neighbor became a short reprieve from the trauma and terror of school. And my brother was there with me, so I had company.

However awful school was, the problems I faced in school were minuscule compared to what I was about to experience at a friend's birthday party.

᷿

I attended birthday parties in the neighborhood. Since those were the only opportunities for social interactions, I gladly went. One particular evening, the birthday celebration was at a family friend's home. I was about five years old. A young teen girl took me to her parents' bedroom. I remember the unimaginable confusion and terror in my mind when she asked me to take all my clothes off. But being five, I followed her instructions. She then asked me to lie on the bed, and she laid over me. I immediately switched off. I remember suffocating, crying, and coughing. She told me that this was what her parents did in their bedroom, which was well beyond my five-year-old mind's understanding. I wasn't supposed to say a word to anyone. With my survival instincts prompting me to escape—the abuse that had already taken place—I put my clothes back on and ran into the living area. I was disheveled and looking for my mom. I found her among the party attendees, however, my voice was stranded inside my vocal cords. I was confused.

My young and innocent mind could not comprehend the depth of what had happened to me, however, I knew I had been violated. I shoved this incident way down in my heart.

Where was Mom? Why was I abused at five years of age by a person of the same gender, on her watch?

I had no idea how this impacted me until I was in therapy in the fourth decade of my life! The people who were supposed to defend me and protect me from such fear and terror and physical abuse in my world were continually failing me, intentionally or perhaps even unintentionally. I felt forgotten and unseen. I became very insecure and untrusting as a child. I experienced both terror and fright a lot during those young years. I was never seen. I learned that my emotions were not to be expressed, so instead, I shut down if they bubbled up. If I expressed emotion, I was laughed and jeered at by Mom, and compared to one of her sisters. I was labeled "a pool of melted butter." I internalized that something was terribly wrong with me. I was "too sensitive" or "too withdrawn," and time and again, I proved her right. I learned I was better off stuffing all of my emotions inside.

⌒

With my brother's medical condition spiraling downhill, my parents were constantly contemplating where to move next. They finally made the decision to return to India. I was six and my brother was close to four. My mother took us back to her parents' home. *Home* for her was her family, her parents, siblings, and the extended family in her hometown. However, I wasn't sure what this meant for me. In any case, this was a temporary release from the prison of childhood I had experienced in Africa.

We went back to Grandpa George and Grandma Sara's house soon thereafter, and I found the same sense of home and belonging that I remembered from my time there before. I thanked God for the familiarity and semblance of what I once experienced as *home*. School became a great outlet to let my hair down. Although I was highly reserved and shy, I aced my classes and stayed at the top of my class. I excelled in academics and even participated in sports—track, long jump, and shot put. Until then, I hadn't realized I had potential, capabilities, or talents of any kind.

My parents spent several long, hard months trying to find jobs in India. I had always heard a lot from my mother and her family about "material scarcity" in my father's home and "plentiful supply" in my mother's home. Soon, Mother found a job, and we moved to a different state in the cooler month of December. Her position was at a private school located on a hill station with chilly temperatures. Daddy moved to South Africa with a new job as well. We stayed on the campus of the residential school where Mother taught. She was now pregnant with my youngest brother and was terribly sick, barely able to get out of bed and unable to care for us. We went without dinner several nights, crying ourselves to sleep. I turned seven without much fanfare or a party. The neighbor baked a cake and brought it over. I was content, as I got to blow out seven lit candles in the dark.

By this time, I compensated for what mother couldn't do due to her morning sickness. I was fully engaged in helping Mom with household chores. Mom would hit the bed as soon as she came home from work, as her morning sickness was getting worse by the day. There was a metallic pipe that hung over the little quadrangle area with a sieve in the ground that served as a sink. I squatted down on the floor and washed dishes that were piled up on the floor, sometimes for over a week or sometimes even two. Many times, I went outside in the early morning and late evening hours in the cold to the main supply well to collect water as we didn't have running water inside. It was right by our house on campus, but what was most difficult was passing by the pigpen with the water buckets. There was one window that opened from our kitchen area out to the view and the stench of that pigpen. To this day, I still wonder what on earth a pigpen was doing in the middle of a school campus.

When I was finished with the dishes and other chores, it felt like an eternity had passed. Mom was passed out, mumbling something on the nights we asked for dinner. Eventually, we just assumed there was no dinner and crawled in the bed next to her and fell asleep.

Soon, we moved into a newer complex on campus which had designated rooms, probably the size of my current suburban master bathroom and closet space. Our new coveted living quarters was a stark contrast to the little dungeon with open bathroom and squatty potty, quadrangle sink, and stove in the corner of the large room. This new duplex was like an upgrade to a fancy hotel. The inside was a safe spot from the stench of the open septic tank still under construction but in full use, as we had working toilets and so did the neighbor in the duplex.

Since Mom was getting closer to her due date with my young-est brother, we returned to my Grandpa George and Grandma Sara's home. There, my youngest brother was born. Grandpa George, with his energetic and fun-loving personality, loved on all of us and played with the new baby, making silly faces and talking his version of baby talk. My loving, entertaining grandpa passed away two months after my youngest brother's birth. My world shattered. Although I was young, I remember the whole week and the funeral. Someone I dearly loved and had deeply connected with had passed away.

I remember having anxiety attacks and wetting my bed for the next several weeks. My head would reel and my heart would race in the middle of the night as if it was going to fly out of my chest. I sat up in bed only to collapse into a ball. Lying in the fetal position, I pulled the covers over me. I had become a pro at suppressing all my emotions around traumatic events as the safest way to navigate my life. I really didn't have another way to express myself. I learned to survive by shoving my emotions deep down until it hurt no more. The only way I knew to cope was to wear masks, pretend like everything was fine, or to sol-dier through.

Mom, my brothers, and I co-slept in the same room. But as I got older, Mother put me in a separate room, and my anxiety attacks became more frequent. The only times I had a break from panic attacks at night were when I slept in the same room as Grandma Sara. During these panic attacks, almost every night as I understand them now, I would wet my bed. I was too embarrassed to tell anyone as this wasn't what other "normal" seven- and eight-year-olds in my class did.

It was around this time when my aunt (dad's only sister who was recovering from surgery) and her children came to live with Grandma Sara. We all made it work and fit into the small 1500-square-foot home. I recall the joy I experienced during this time, as this was by far one of the most memorable and happiest times of my childhood. My cousins, my brother, and I played in the yard, climbed trees, and plucked fruits, caught butterflies, and explored the ferns, thistles, and bushes, as we were back in the tropical environment.

Life quickly changed. We were transitioning to living essentially as a multi-generational family, which wasn't culturally unusual during that time period. I gladly took on a lot of responsibility, being the oldest of all the children. I turned into "little mommy" as our mothers were post-surgery (my aunt) and post-birth (my mom). I was responsible at school as well as at home and found myself continually excelling at school work and extracurricular activities. I topped the class despite having to learn a new language since English was my first language at the time. I turned into a good little girl who earned good grades and was highly responsible. Daddy found a job soon after in Swaziland in southern Africa.

I assisted with caring for all the younger children as much as I could. Grandma Sara needed help around the home, including daily living needs, kids' activities, and chores around the house. Every morning, I carried four backpacks, lunches, and water bottles on my shoulders as I walked with my cousins and my brother down the dirt road to wait for the school bus. Our lives continued in our small town in my father's family home in India for another school year. Mother soon found a job at a local school. We, all the cousins, went together to the school where she taught. Grandma Sara watched the baby with the assistance of a helper. Eventually, my aunt and her family returned to her husband in another state after she fully recovered from surgery. I began to miss my caring and nurturing aunt and my cousins terribly—a little piece of home left with them. The proverbial rug was pulled out from under me again.

While we lived with my Grandma Sara, she woke up at four in the morning every day, spent a good hour in prayer, then cooked breakfast and lunch. When we woke up, our lunches were packed, and she fed us all breakfast and milk. She insisted we drink a cup of milk so we could grow! Soon I was learning to cook with Grandma Sara. I am so thankful for those opportunities I had with her, to learn how to cook authentic South Indian meals. I was able to cut vegetables just like my grandma and put a meal on the table by the age of eight.

This was our new life. This was *home*. We adjusted into our new roles. I took on the role of a responsible, good little girl who did what she needed to do. My brother continued with his illness, and Mom went back to her old patterns of worry and fear. She spent her time worrying, at the market, or busy outside the home with "a project." Grandma Sara stepped into the primary role of watching, nurturing, and "mothering" us all.

I began to explore God in my eight-year-old mind. At this time, he felt very close to me in the absence of my earthly father who was separated from us by time and distance. At this point, my father was still working overseas in Africa, trying to make ends meet, and providing for the family. God was a good Father, I tangibly felt him during prayer time through music and my love for singing.

Unseen and Forgotten?

Maybe I had finally begun to feel somewhat at home and found *Mom* in my loving Grandma Sara. Maybe home is where you make it! Yet, who was my mom to me? Was she just a person who gave birth to me and brought me into this world?

~⊙~

Reflection Questions

Have you felt orphaned or abandoned by someone who was supposed to be a nurturer, caretaker, and protector, even though they might have provided a roof over your head?

Have you felt neglected because of the family environment, displacement of family, or because of the lack of emotional health of the family that you were placed in?

Have you had any positive experiences with another family that you dearly hung on to, hoping they would fill your need for a primary parental relationship? Did this relationship end up being temporary? Or maybe it didn't turn out the way you expected?

Have you had to be the scapegoat child or surrogate parent to younger siblings or others in the household who were younger than you?

Can you think of one or more individuals who stood in the gap for you and provided you with loving relationships, even for brief periods along your life's journey?

~◦~

Words of encouragement

I had experienced abandonment and neglect, whether it was being put out in the dark or left alone at home, and I didn't deserve it. If you have experienced this, you don't deserve it either. If you have been through experiences of abandonment, neglect, or lack of nurture and protection, it was not your fault nor was it because of you!

Please hear me—our parents were here before us and they have a God-given responsibility to nurture and protect the children they chose to bring into this world. Any form of abuse has no place and cannot be justified.

Mentally and emotionally, I eventually had to put the responsibility where it belonged.

As hard as it is to accept, I was not **alone in my soul wounding,** *God was with me, and he was and is with you!*

~⊙~

Final Note

If you process pain in a healthy way, God can use the broken circumstances of your life and those you consider your offenders to heal you. Just hang in there—hang on to that sliver of hope in Him. He can and will use everything for your restoration and his Glory!

A broken family system doesn't need to define whether God was with you or for you. There is another way besides a broken way to freedom. He can use your brokenness to heal you.

Chapter 4

✺

UNTOUCHED?

*"But whoso shall offend one of these little ones
which believe in me, it were better for him that
a millstone were hanged about his neck, and
that he were drowned in the depth of the sea."*
—Matthew 18:6 (KJV)

No child deserves to be violated in any form. Here, I will walk you through my agony and powerlessness as a child. I was oblivious to the emotional violations that I had experienced, which eventually led to more of my innocence being stolen. *If these events are triggering for you, please take action as I've encouraged at the end of this chapter.*

✺

My father was visiting us the following summer (he was still working in Swaziland in Southern Africa). I was so thrilled to have him back for a couple of months, as he was off from school and teaching for the summer break. It felt a little strange initially to reconnect, however, I quickly grew accustomed to his presence again.

Since music was very dear to my heart, my father took me to music lessons.

"Do you want to become a musician?" Daddy asked.

"I can?"

"Yes, you can be anything you want to be, you just need to train for it," he said.

"Really?" I was so amazed and greatly overjoyed that my daddy thought I could become anything I dreamed of.

"Do you want to start some lessons in piano?" he asked.

My instant answer was an emphatic, "Yes. Yes. Yes."

"Okay, then. Let's do it."

Daddy signed me up and took me to music lessons with a music teacher who played the grand piano at the local church (and who was also a family member). We had to take public transportation to get to his house. He lived by the side of a canal off the beaten path from the bus stop. I was so excited. Somebody believed something about me—that I had potential. In fact, my father told me that I could become anything if I set my heart to it. But I had to dream first. And then I had to practice! I was determined to give it everything I had. I remembered all the times I hung out with the organist at the school chapel the previous year. He told Mother I sang so well and had attempted to convince her to send me for voice and piano lessons. Here it was finally—I was pumped for my next adventure. Music!

Daddy soon returned to his job overseas. This time, my mother accompanied him. One particular summer afternoon after they had left, Grandma Sara took me to my music teacher. Then she left with his wife to go see their new home under construction across the road from a canal that wrapped around the side of the acreage. The current home where I was to take my lessons was situated remotely in a thicket of trees, quite isolated. It was an old, dingy home, with what little lights there were merely lighting the living area. The only other lighting was through the high, tiny windows that let the skylight in. Suddenly, the lights turned dim and then off. I knew in my young innocent heart that some dark, impending doom was looming and just about to come upon me.

I didn't suspect any act of violence since this man had appeared kindhearted and showed great concern for me. He empathized with how lonely it must have been without my father around. Since he played the piano at church during the worship service, I did not assume anything other than that he was kind and caring. He had filled the "daddy hole" in my heart and the deficit in my need for loving and nurturing developmental touch. He engaged in conversation about my parents, especially about how isolating it must feel with daddy away overseas.

This particular day (about a year into my lessons), he overlooked all my mistakes. He showered me with generous compliments about my skill level and how awesome I played the March tunes. Little did I know, he was "grooming" me.

Before I even realized what was happening, he came up very close, rubbed close to my side, and began putting his hands over mine as I played the piece of music he had set out for me that day. Hand over hand, his forearms over mine, enveloping me with his bigger and stronger chest, he transported me into another world. Music broke the silence around me. I was in heaven.

I couldn't believe what my ears heard—I had come so far with my skill level. I smelled his breath very close to my face, and my heart began to thump as he asked me to stop playing the piano. *That was a brisk move.* He gestured for me to come sit on his lap after he pulled up a footstool close to the piano.

There was an eerie silence in the room. I began to feel light headed. My vision blurred. It felt as if all the blood was draining out of my body. I thought I was surely going to black out for no reason. I felt terrified and suddenly frozen.

He kept turning, looking back through the small window across the hall from us. With a smirk on his face, a smile breaking out of the corner of his lips—sly and clandestine written all over his face—he began describing my best friend's body. At that point, I put two and two together—now it made complete sense as to why she had abruptly quit piano classes. What on earth was I hearing? He told me that he would explain "everything" to me in just a minute. As he violated me, I froze right down to the core of my being. My heart still pounding—rattling against my rib cage, about to burst and fly out of my chest—I tried to mentally prepare myself to run, punch, kick, and scream. But I couldn't move. Then it all stopped. I couldn't breathe, I felt as if an elephant was sitting on my chest. I was positive I was going to faint and then die. The stench of the old man was too much to bear.

Nauseated, immobilized by fear and shame and guilt (even though I had done nothing wrong), I tried to put my bare feet to the ground and sprint. It took me nowhere—I couldn't move. I was aphonic, my vocal cords felt paralyzed. I heard brisk footsteps approaching the house; Grandma Sara and the old man's wife were returning. I came back to my senses. I quickly took my clothes off the ground and threw them back on. A cloud of shame enveloped me. What just happened? All I knew was I wanted to hide and never be seen again. When Grandma Sara walked in, I felt naked and exposed, even with clothes on. I couldn't shake off the feeling of a thousand crawling creatures making their way up my body. I was afraid Grandma Sara would walk in and find me in this state.

I cried a little. He told me I was never to say a word to anyone. And he would see me back again for lessons. I did not utter a word and did return for lessons—weekly.

From then on, every time I put my hand on the piano, a fog came over me. I couldn't remember anything I learned, nor could I ever think clearly in piano classes again. I just had to quit. Yet I went to lessons week after week. I was reprimanded by my piano teacher for losing all the skills I had learned over the past two years.

One day, I broke down and told Grandma Sara about the events that transpired at my music teacher's house that day. I was determined to make sure I gave minimal details as I coldly told Grandma Sara my story. I wondered what Grandma Sara thought of me? Was I somehow in the wrong?

To my surprise, Grandma Sara was furious and upset all at the same time. That was the end of my stint with music. She called the teacher's wife and broke the news to her. I have no idea what she told her or how much she disclosed. All that mattered to me was that Grandma Sara had executed some justice on my behalf, but I still had a lot of revenge pending. Who would stand up for me?

A couple of years later, Mom told me she knew of "something" that happened to me in music classes. I dismissed the conversation, as I knew from experience that Mom was not good at keeping anything to herself. Unfortunately, she did violate my confidence and spread this news to other family members.

When I was twelve, Mom told me that I had to accompany her to visit this relative. He was in the hospital and dying. I thought to myself, *Perhaps God punished him for violating me as a child*. I told Mother that I was uncomfortable visiting him. Yet, Mother re-traumatized me by taking me back to the man who had violated me. I cringed. I felt naked again. Mother knew that I had been sexually violated by him. I just didn't know *how much* she knew. I was determined not to engage in conversation with him. As I verbally protested my hesitancy to accompany her, she reminded me how terrible, inconsiderate, and uncompassionate I was being to the old man who had sexually abused me. My heart raced. I felt nauseated as I staggered down the hallway to hospital room 218 on hallway A. My mother convinced me that the godly thing I *had to do* was to go see him in his misery.

Once again, I felt all the blood leave my face and my head. I could smell the old man's stench from a few feet away. Mother insisted that I go stand by the man's bedside and talk to him. I felt naked and violated all over again—many, many times over again. While he stared at me from head to toe, mother was clearly inspecting the emotions that lined my face. Since I learned to survive by shoving all my emotions in, I swallowed it all up one more time—the shame, guilt, and character assassination for not showing up at the door of my abuser to face him. Mother was literally making me relive the abuse, re-traumatizing me. Why didn't Mom realize what she was doing to me? At that moment, as intense shame washed over me, I wondered if the emotional abuse and psychological trauma that she inflicted upon me that day were deliberate and intentional… I would have been better off dead than to suffer intentional harm at the hands of my own mother.

The violation by my music teacher was minuscule compared to the secondary trauma Mother inflicted upon me.

> *The many times I heard her share my story with others in front of me reinforced and convinced my young mind that somehow something was terribly wrong with me.*

I was untouchable, less than, not of value or of worth. I was dirty—damaged goods. I wished some protective and non-deceiving part of my mother was around to rescue me.

◞

The next year, I was sent to boarding school, around age thirteen. With a new job, my mother once again left to join my father. My younger brother was sent to my uncle's (father's brother) house after staying with Grandma Sara for a year. My youngest sibling went to live with my parents. Vulnerable, alone, and unprotected, I experienced several abusive and traumatic events that became part of my existence.

*It only takes a few minutes of
an adult's violation to mar and
damage a child for a lifetime.*

I did not have anyone in my life—a safe place—to unload the silent cries of my soul. I once told my mom about another incident. It traveled around and across the globe to extended family. I was told how my character was similar to someone dear to her who was violated—blaming me for what happened because of my naivety and insular disposition. Yes, I was extremely withdrawn, betrayed by the people who were supposed to love, protect, and advocate for me. But instead of understanding, I was met with disbelief and indifference from Mom. Mother was not a safe confidant for me. I had the saving grace of my Grandma Sara with whom I had the closest relationship. In her eighty-year-old wisdom, she modeled trustworthiness, confidentiality, and safety as valuable traits that I embraced.

Obviously, I developed huge trust issues with Mom. She was the last person I confided in. And then one day, later in life when my own daughter was about five years old, I was talking with Mother. She was discussing strained relationships in the family and touched on the subject of abuse! Mom wondered if my daughter had ever been violated by anyone in the family? Why would I even be asked such a question? I told her that my daughter had "enough relationship with me" that she would disclose everything to me if such a thing, God forbid, happened. Mother told me that she was glad I *was never* sexually violated.

That day, everything within me welled up to the point that I began fuming out my ears. The whole world came to a standstill. Once more, I snapped at her. At the age of thirty-five, I was adamant that this God-ordained person who gave birth to me would not minimize what was done to me, nor would she stand in the way of whatever I needed to start my healing journey. Was Mom's patterns of minimizing, shaming, and retraumatizing me and my story due to self-loathing herself? It felt as if what happened to me did not matter to Mom, as if it was not serious enough or true enough for her. Did Mom have a story too, I wondered? Perhaps mine was a trigger and she escaped by minimizing and denying. But I decided I was going to deal with the truth of my story. I just didn't know how.

Three decades later, through counseling, recovery groups, and by replacing my broken tapes with truth from God's word, I began the journey of renewing my mind.

❧

Reflection Questions

Is there a time in your life when you felt you were physically neglected? A time when you did not receive the healthy, loving, and nurturing non-sexual touch that you needed to develop as a normal human being?

How does that make you feel?

Have you felt totally unseen by the people who were supposed to protect, love, and advocate for you through traumatic events?

Have you been shamed for abuse of any kind that happened to you? Have you seen yourself as worthless or damaged goods due to violations including emotional, physical, and/or sexual abuse? Have you ever been made to feel that you contributed to these events and you were somehow responsible?

Do you have flesh-and-blood safe relationships in your life with people who reside in your zip code that you can share your innermost wounding with?

∽

Words of encouragement

If you are in a situation where there is emotional/verbal, physical, or sexual abuse, seek help immediately. If you are a teen or a young adult and you have been threatened to keep silent, do not comply. You can call one of the numbers I provide in the resources at the end of the book.

Seek immediate help from a safe adult, and please seek immediate counseling. Do not let your parent(s) tell you it is too shameful, and do not take threats as a deterrent from seeking help.

Find a counselor trained in the area of these types of abuse. Find support in a trusted friend or support group. Silence will not help you.

At ten years old, I thought and felt that God avenged these violations against me. I believed God was working out his vengeance against my offenders. I had read in scripture that our battles belong to the Lord! But this didn't make any sense to me. These experiences and the shame associated with them killed me on the inside for years. I couldn't take this journey up on my own. Childhood sexual abuse can lead to depression. It can compromise your immune system and even cause you to have a chronic illness. Studies have shown that these types of abuse can hold your thought patterns and emotions hostage even into the sixth and seventh decades of life.[3]

*Later in my adult life, I still felt **untouched**, unseen by my mother and unseen by God. The biblical story of Hagar spoke to me so deeply as I turned to scripture for comfort. Hagar was put out in the desert with a child. Sarah, her mistress, disliked her. Sarah was not kind to her and mistreated her because Sarah herself was unable to have children. Sarah was jealous of Hagar because Hagar bore Abraham the child that Sarah thought she would. Sarah couldn't face her own pain. Instead, she turned against Hagar. Can you imagine the loss of purpose Hagar experienced? She even had a child outside of marriage that she had to raise who was not a part of her own will and purpose.*

*I carried these wounds of abuse into my adulthood, so much so that they translated into my unworthy feelings of being **untouchable** and unseen by my husband.*

⌒

Final Note

There is a God who sees us right in the pit of where we are. He is touched by our sadness and our loss. What has broken your heart breaks his heart. His name is, "I am... the God who sees." The parts of me another woman (my mom and other mother figures in my life) and even my husband couldn't see, God could see. Jesus healed and comforted people tangibly with His presence. We need tangible people around us who see us and understand us. There is no way around it. We need to be seen, heard, and believed. Jesus touched people with His presence and His words of life. There are people around you that God has put in your life, in community, for healing in this way. Identify them. You are not damaged goods or untouchable. You don't need to survive in isolation. Nothing is wrong with you.

I was brainwashed for a long period of my life after being told that the offenses weren't too bad (minimizing it), that it wasn't sexual abuse (invalidating my pain), and that something was inherently wrong with me because of what was done to me. That was a lie from the pit of hell! I had to separate my "who" (I am bad or something is wrong with me) from my "do" (something was done to me or I did something wrong). The shame and false guilt did not belong to me. If you are experiencing shame and guilt, what has been done to you does not define who you are and whom you are created to be. **Own your pain, but not your shame.** *Period. Break your silence. Reach out for help. You are totally worthy of help and healing.*

Chapter 5

⟡

UNHEARD AND VOICE LOST

*"No person is your friend (or kin) who demands
your silence, or denies your right to grow and
be perceived as fully blossomed as you were
intended. Or who belittles in any fashion the
gifts you labor so to bring into the world."*

— Alice Walker

I agree with Alice Walker. I will explain how my voice was stolen, and how I walked into adulthood carrying the lie that I was unworthy of being heard.

As I mentioned in the last chapter, not only was my story minimized, but I felt my emotions were unseen for three and a half decades; I believed I did not matter to Mom. I felt that way from the time I was a child. Therefore, it felt outlandish to expect anything different as an adult. My poor mom was enmeshed in a codependent network that enabled her and provided a fuel supply of narcissistic energy. Her mind swayed whichever way the wind blew, receiving her self-worth and self-image from that network of influence. And they fed off her stories, including those from my life.

My dad, on the other hand, recognized my creative inclination for art, in addition to my musical interests. He believed in me. Remember, Daddy told me I could become anything I wanted—an artist, a musician, or anything I put my mind to!

∾

The summer Daddy returned, I tried my hand at art—water coloring. It was like fresh water on the dry and parched land of my mind, devoid of any positive input or affirmation. I competed in a local art competition and won. Although I was in fifth grade, the coordinator for the event (who was also a distant family member with ill feelings against my family) deliberately placed me in a higher category. I won third place in the eighth- through tenth-grade age group because of the work I produced. Dad told me that he believed I would have won first place if I was placed in the correct category; third through fifth grade. *How unfair!*, I thought. Dad did take it up with the coordinators later. Their apology did not satisfy me, as I had lost an opportunity to be placed to compete at the state level. However, I basked in Dad's affirmations.

I tried voice lessons and singing next, and I loved it. In fifth grade, I practiced a song for an upcoming school competition, preparing every line until I perfected my pitch. I even took voice lessons, and I was finally ready. I entered the big stage of the large school auditorium to perform in front of the entire school. I felt confident as I walked up to the stage. After all, Mom was in the audience to support me, everything was going to be just fine.

Then it happened. As I started to sing, I completely forgot every word, my mind drawing a blank as the words stuck in my vocal cords. My terrified gaze rapidly moved across the auditorium, scanning every aisle and row. I finally spotted Mom. I quickly became paralyzed by this funny belly laughter that arose from her. Throngs of people surrounding her poked fun at me. As I stood there frozen in disbelief (with my words swallowed up), I reinstated the thought, What a terrible failure you are.

The room went dark, and I felt like I would pass out at any moment. Someone walked up to me, took me by the hand, and walked me off the stage. My whole world came to a standstill, yet again. I felt intense shame—that cloud of shame, which was so familiar, like a waterfall pouring over me from a bucket that flipped upside down. I wanted to bury my head in the sand and never come out. Not only did I lose my words that day, but I also lost my voice.

꩜

Mother made me sign up for every stage competition after that to "fix me." Oration and singing. She knew I had a problem. Without fail, I was signed up for the next event and the next. I continued to lose any sense of worth, afraid that I would never use my voice again. I began to believe that my pitch was frozen and that I could never sing high notes again. What a lie!

Lack of confidence stayed with me as a perpetual issue. I spent hours researching and preparing, yet never feeling confident about my abilities or talents. This became a debilitating anxiety I dealt with socially. Family members commented about my voice when I spoke, as I began to have a sunken look with my face and head held down. I used a low, monotonous voice that was barely audible. Many people commented on my social awkwardness, posture, and lack of confidence. Some even prayed as though there was a demon on the inside of me that needed to be chased out.

∽

As I processed my childhood traumatic events in therapy, I discovered that before cognitive thought processes kicked in, I went into modes of fear, panic, and shut down as the flight, fight, or freeze responses kicked in for survival. Somewhere along the way, my primitive emotional brain—my limbic system—learned to kick into overdrive before my thinking brain went online. I learned that multiple traumas over time, along with big 'T' traumas, were playing their dirty little game in my life.

In order to heal, I decided I needed to identify each traumatic event; name, feel, and process the emotions; identify the lies that I believed, and replace them with truth statements.

For me, that included God's word and what the Bible had to say about me. I was going to give it a try! What did I have to lose, after all?

And so, I started the journey of acknowledging, owning, and naming my pain; then, disowning it and replacing it with truth statements. But when it came to speaking with Mom, or my other mothering crew, I would find myself right back at square one. Right where I began: the scared little girl who was supposed to be good and perfect. The go-to scapegoat that was scorned, shamed, belittled, labeled, and put in my place.

Even as a grown adult, I always walked away questioning myself: *Who do you think you are?* Or, *how dare you?* I clearly had a lot of work to do.

I finally decided to wear my new wardrobe: *My truth statements*. I identified each lie that played on repeat in my head. For each lie that I identified with words, I wrote down a truth statement to combat that lie. I struggled even as an adult with those lies rolling around in my head as a grown woman—that I lost my voice, my singing voice, my talking voice. I let others speak for me because I had lost all confidence in my abilities. I looked to scripture for answers. I came across Hannah of the Bible who felt unheard by God. While Hannah was destitute—with all her hope stolen—a woman named Paneana kicked her in the gut with sarcastic and piercing words. Hannah was so overcome by emotions that, by the time she arrived at the temple to pray to her God, her voice was only capable of indecipherable groaning. The priest Eli thought she was drunk, yet he granted her request.

What a beautiful imagery of God honoring her request, even when Hannah could barely speak, groaning in her lament. In the New Testament, the Spirit gives us utterances like groans when we don't have words. Who is this Spirit? This the Helper, the Comforter, who came alongside Hannah and gave her words. This same Spirit is available to you and me. He gives us words. They may begin with a groan, but if you let him, he will eventually give you words. He will guide you into all truth, providing truth statements as you need.

It is ironic that God would call me into a helping profession—a Speech-Language Pathologist—someone who helps the voiceless and the communication impaired find their voice. My work wasn't done. I told myself I would serve people. I would serve in society somehow.

∽

Reflection Questions

Was there a time in your life when you felt unheard? Unheard by a parent, a spouse, or someone significant in your life?

Was your grief and frustration so overwhelming that you couldn't speak to another human being because you knew they wouldn't understand you, or much worse, would misunderstand you?

Do you believe you can be heard in this world?

∽

Words of encouragement

Do you have any "Eli's" in your life? We need our "Eli's," we need community, we need a tribe, co-sufferers, co-warriors, and co-victors to walk with us on our journeys of life. Don't stay a victim, or in a co-victim group. Find a co-victor group of people who know victory and the Victor!

~⊙~

Final Note

The fact that I am writing this book is proof that I have battled the lies and found my voice. I believed for a very long time that if I took inventory of my heart or my heart's condition and wrote it down, it would be too real; hence, I refused to write. I would have to face my reality if I wrote it down. In the Psalms, David took an inventory of his heart, and he let God examine his heart and bring to his mind the things he needed to face. Truth is your birthright! Speak it! Write it! Scream it from the rooftops! Speak it to your soul as David did in the Psalms. Do whatever it takes until you have found your truth and that truth begins to feel comfortable, replacing the lies that you have believed.

The very thing that was stolen away from me, my voice, is being redeemed through the pages of this book. If He can redeem it for me, he can and will for you too! Let him do this for you; take the first step and reach out for help

Conclusion to Part I - Purpose Stolen

What childhood traumatic events and early dysfunction do to people is against the very fabric of their humanity. I am not a theologian, psychologist, or counselor, nor is it my intent to feminize a higher power that I call God. I wrote these pieces of my story down, not out of fear or victimhood but to shift my mental narrative by getting in touch with my vulnerability and writing about unjust things that happened to me. Ultimately, though, these events do not need to define us when we seek help to work on past trauma.

I want to offer you hope—that the stories of your past or what was done to you, even by the people closest to you, don't need to define who you are. We need to face our pain. When we face our histories of soul wounding and become aware of personal issues that contribute to our problems in the present, we have crossed our biggest hurdle. Then we need to reach out for help. As the poet, Leonard Cohen states, "Ring the bells that still can ring. Forget your perfect offering. There is a crack in everything. That's how the light gets in."

PART II:

❦

CREATED ON PURPOSE

~⌾

Introduction to Part II

As a young child, I was dependent on my primary caregivers—emotionally, physically, and spiritually—to
nurture, care for, and protect me from the chaos in my
young, often dangerous world. This section is about my realization of what it should have been, what it was supposed
to look like.

We are all born with a hard drive that is perfectly wired
for connection, community, and safety. In our childlike
innocence, there was no fear of the future, but instead
playfulness, joy, and curiosity. For some of us, when we
experienced childhood trauma, separation, abandonment, or
neglect from people in our lives, our family systems, and
many other systems, our brains rewrote some of that hard
wiring. So, some of us inherited a new dysfunctional code,
riddled with viruses.

In this section, I simply chose to recognize those things
that needed repair (even with early attachment figures in my
life refusing to make amends) so I could redeem my purpose.

Chapter 6

❦

THE SACRED PLACE

"The two most important days in your life are the day you are born, and the day you find out why."

—Mark Twain

"Before the mountains were born or You gave birth to the earth and the world, even from ever-lasting to everlasting you are [the eternal] God."

—Psalm 90:2 (AMP)

"For he knows how we are formed, he remembers that we are dust."

—Psalm 103:14 (NIV)

When I was in my lowest moments, contemplating if life was worth living, God gently whispered to my spirit only what He could in those moments. And thus, I applied and interpreted the key scriptures above in my life.

✑

I had just accepted my first job after graduating with a master's degree in Speech-Language Pathology and Audiology from the top university for my profession in India. This happened just as I was stepping into the second millennium, putting me on cloud nine! It was a surprise to many that I secured admission in the first place because they thought I wasn't "smart enough."

I didn't skip a beat. Within one week of graduating, I interviewed for a job and had my offer letter in hand to work as a speech-language pathologist at the Institute for Cognitive and Communicative Neurosciences. I loved studying the brain (and behaviors associated) all through my undergraduate and graduate programs. Here, at my feet, was the perfect job to put into practice everything I had learned in school. I was so drawn to the work I did: the research involved, the brain science, and working with a multidisciplinary team, including a neurologist. I even learned how to read an MRI and an EEG.

A year into my working career, my mom sent word that due to a serious illness, she required surgery, without which she would eventually die. After Mother had her surgery, the surgeon called me and my aunt to show us her uterus before she sent it for biopsy. She was concerned that my mom did have cancer. I wondered how many people had the opportunity to literally see their mother's womb as an adult. Strangely, I did. Not by my choice, but by circumstance. The psalmist talks about how we are fearfully and wonderfully made and knit together in our mother's womb—hemmed from behind and before.[4] The thought struck me hard; if not for my mother's womb, I wouldn't be here. What a mystery!

I was looking at where my life began in the sacred space of my mother's womb—my home—where she gave me life and nourishment for nine months before my arrival into this world. As I witnessed this strange piece of my physical biology on a plastic platter, God ministered to my heart, and I reflected on the sacredness of the space I was carefully weaved in by unseen and mighty hands—the only space where I was created and could thrive for my first nine months.

Following the surgery, in her delirious state of mind and in our private moments together, Mother read me her diary. In case she died of cancer, she had unfinished business with Grandma Sara and others on my father's side of the family. With determination, she voiced her disappointments, regrets, and anger to me. She felt betrayed that her children were taken from her. For the first time, I realized she had traumatic events and memories from the past haunting her, in addition to the current big Trauma of fighting for her life.

Goodness, gracious! Was I going to lose Mom right along with the warm and cozy space I was conceived in? Was she dying? It was a paradoxical thought I didn't want to entertain. I barely heard the doctor's mutterings about the possible cancer diagnosis, as I was lost in the intrigue and mystery of my mother's womb sitting in the hands of the surgeon standing right in front of me!

God birthed the earth and all that live in it. God is the Creator of the womb and the Creator of everything. He created our inmost being in the secret and sacred place of the womb. He knew us before he laid the foundations of the earth. I thought about that for a moment. As he was planning out the design of the earth, the far foundations and stretches and expanse of the heavens, he was also thinking about my form. He saw my unformed body in his mind! This blew me away. I stood there on the cusp of losing my mom, yet lost in awe and wonder.

But I, too, had unfinished business with my mother. I struggled to reconcile my thoughts about our relationship with all that God was unfolding before my eyes—his awareness of me, his purposeful use of my mother's womb. But who was I to understand the mind of God?

I had made valid conclusions with my own intellect that were fairly reasonable. I was angry with Mom, but I did not want her to die. I had a choice to believe it or not. That the God I had experienced as a child (something or someone bigger than me—my spiritual space) had to bring it together.

My depressed mind began feeling suicidal. I remembered the last time I felt this way. God woke people up in the middle of the night to pray for me, specifically to preserve my life from suicidal thoughts. In my suicidal moment, I was reminded of his faithfulness in preserving my life in the past. This time, I hung on to the visualization of the sacred space of the womb—a safe, hidden, secret, dark chamber, a sacred space where I was created. A hidden place, warm and tucked away in a private chamber. The creator didn't even require light to weave and hem me from behind and under as he framed my unformed body.

Deep in my spirit, I had the following revelation: I didn't have a choice as to which womb would bring me into this world. It didn't matter how I got here. I was created by someone who was familiar with the design and matters of the womb.

In the book of Job, He uses the design of the womb for creation—the seas burst forth from the abyss of the womb (Job 38:8) and even before he laid the foundations of the earth, He had you on his mind.

That was hard to wrap my head around. God trusted a woman's womb, the secret place, to send his only son—who was fully God, yet fully human, helpless at birth, just like any one of us. If God created me in my mother's womb, then he certainly had to be familiar with the design. Just like an architect creates by design, God had my DNA all aligned and sorted. My traits, my personality, the color of my hair, my eyes, and my skin—the whole package. I couldn't help but believe that I was not created by chance! In His creation story, there was the laying of the foundations of the earth God created on purpose. He created on purpose and the sacred space he was creating in—the matters of the womb. Could this reflect the Mother-ness of God?

God's word in Psalm 139:5 reveals to us this truth that from the beginning to the end he formed us and set his hand upon us. God is a creator. He is familiar with the sacred matters of the space that he is creating, so I decided I would leave the creation story in my womb to the God of the Universe.

I hung on to the thought "He created me by design, on purpose, for a purpose."

Maybe I was just bent on the idea from 1 Corinthians 2:19 that tells us that no eye has seen, no ear has heard, and no human mind has conceived the things that God has prepared for those who love him. His thoughts and ways are higher than mine. Isaiah 55:8-9 (NIV) says, "For my thoughts are not your thoughts neither are your ways my ways declares the Lord as the heavens are higher than the earth so are my ways higher than your ways and my thoughts than your thoughts." These verses sustained me. I had a purpose. I still had no idea what it all meant, but I chose to hang on to these thoughts; my life actually had purposeful meaning.

In this deep, revelatory moment in my mother's hospital room, God also reminded me of the creation story in Genesis. In Hebrew, the word "bara" means to *create*. Genesis means *beginning* or *origin*. In the beginning, God created the substance of the heavens and the earth—he created, by design, the world and he created man. I was his idea, even before he laid the foundations of the earth he saw my unformed body.

For we are God's workmanship created in Christ Jesus to do good works, which God prepared in advance as our way of life. After this experience, I had to believe God had a plan for me, including motherhood.

Reflection Questions

Have you asked yourself, like I did, if God made a huge mistake in creating you?

Have you ever felt your purpose in this life was stolen by others?

As a little child, did you dream of the future? Did you dream of becoming someone?

What were those dreams, if any?

~⌒~

Words of encouragement

I believed a lie that I was created by accident. That I was a mistake. That the world would have been better off without me. I had to own and acknowledge these feelings as a result of my sense of abandonment, however painful it was. I had to acknowledge that I had childhood trauma wounds from neglect and abandonment. I had to name them, own them, process them, and then disown them.

I had to find and speak my truths and replace the lies that I had believed and carried with me for many decades. And so can you!

My inner core, the spiritual parts of me, had to learn to wear truths that I found in God's word. Initially, they were ill-fitting. It didn't feel right after wearing something else for so long, but I had to make a choice to wear truth anyway. And so can you!

If you can't think of any dreams from your past, I invite you to dare to dream again, wherever you are in life, whatever your circumstances. Create a vision board with your purpose and add answers to your questions along the way, as I did.

∾

Final Note

I had to learn to believe, all over again, that I was born with endless possibilities. I had to make a choice to believe and dream again, that I could be restored.

We were created and wired for connection—neurologically, biologically, socially, and spiritually. In the next chapter, I will elaborate on what I've learned about connection and how we, as humans, were born wired for connection. I invite you to imagine, reflect, and connect with that infant sense of yourself, full of potential and endless possibilities when you were born. Connection, which is a deep sense of security and familiarity with others and God from birth, is your birthright.

Chapter 7

ᥫ

WIRED FOR CONNECTION AND CREATED FOR INTIMACY

"The propensity to make strong emotional bonds to particular individuals is a basic component of human nature."
—John Bowlby

"Attachment is a unifying principle that reaches from the biological depths of our being to its furthest spiritual reaches."
— Jeremy Homes, John Bowlby

I was standing at the threshold of my future, the long journey ahead into the greatest calling of my life—motherhood. Yet again, I was frightened with the undercurrent of my early traumatic events weaving through my life's journey. I began to see

105

it through the lens of my child, the beautiful daughter that I had just brought into this world. My daughterhood was triggered. I was holding my own child and wondering who I was to my mother. Was I just a fantasy, a wisp, or an imaginary daughter? Was this an imaginary bonding I shared with her? This chapter will walk you through my search for answers to these questions.

◎

Mom mothered her younger sisters, as she was the oldest of her siblings. Ironically, she even called me all of their names, every one of them, including her brothers, before arriving at mine! As a young child, I frequently wondered why she was so consumed with them all the time, even to the point of addressing me by the wrong gender before she could utter my name. I wondered if I had somehow disappeared from her world. Her words about my birth story frequently popped in my mind. I remembered how Mom was convinced I looked like one of her younger sisters. I was beautiful like her, but then I turned dark (ugly) quickly. At least, that is how I perceived it. Mom was intentionally present for and connected with her sisters, which was the dire opposite of our relationship. They were a codependent group, enmeshed in a tangle of issues, with unhealthy connections and attachments to each other. Although, I think they truly believed they were helping each other.

As I held and experienced my infant daughter, I continued to ponder and learn how she was wired for connection, how humans are pre-wired for connection. God began settling some things in my heart. I was my daughter's nurturer. I kept her alive, warm, fed, and comforted. There was something unique and different about this mother-child bond. She was a helpless infant, totally dependent on me, on my body, for sustenance and nutrition. As I continued to experience motherhood with my daughter, it was set in stone for me—babies are wired for connection. All the classes I took in school about child development; emotional, social, language, and physical milestones were now unfolding in real life with my growing baby.

God was ministering to my heart deeply, reminding me of the following truths. If you are human, you arrived into this world through a mother. You were conceived in your mother's womb, and she gave birth to you! That is the only way you arrived on this planet.

Love and belonging, nurture and security are any human being's top needs. We have a soul, mind, and spirit. We are all born with an innate instinct for security, connection, and intimacy. The first life-giving connections begin in the womb as the mother provides nourishment. The baby is connected to the mother in vitro. What she eats, what she thinks, and what she speaks does impact the baby. There are countless stories of babies in orphanages who die from deprivation of connection through touch, sight, or sound to another human being. This is called "failure to thrive." We have been created with five senses that are alive and well regardless of our circumstances. God gave us these senses with the primitive purpose to connect with the world around us. According to research, even NICU babies who are highly fragile thrive through holding time, hearing the mother's heartbeat (or the father's), and skin to skin contact. This baseline blueprint for wiring stays with us for life. However, over time, many factors can disrupt this imprint; parental nurture, social, cultural, and dysfunctional parenting that transmitted over the generations.

We learn this connection continuously from our parents, and we take it into our adult relationships including our spouses and significant others. We seek relationships for intimacy through secure, emotionally connected, and relational ways. We need support from others in our lives who see us for who we are, without judgment. There is healing in empathetic connection.

As a stay-at-home mom, I watched my children as they demonstrated how we humans are wired for connection. I got to spend intentional, deliberate time with both of my children. I concluded that what I had known about the five senses is very alive in the first two years of life. We are physically, neurologically, and spiritually wired for intimacy. Research shows that even in the case of a traumatic event, the amount of support, empathy, and connection we have with trustworthy and emotionally safe people can improve our success for healing. If we have early wounds shoved deep down that we haven't processed, we are still living with them. They rear their ugly heads in our adult lives. I began to realize that what appeared to be my independence at a very young age was in reality "detachment."

I experienced severe emotional detachment from people and the world around me. Detachment and disconnection were survival skills that I learned to avoid getting hurt in relationships, for self-preservation. The wounds of disconnection from my early years on this planet translated to insecurity, fear, and emotional protection. I was unable to receive any form of affection for years. Yes, even from a very young age. I literally used the palms of my hands to wipe off any demonstration of affection like a kiss or a hug. I cringed with every physical embrace. I did not receive compliments. I kept everyone, including friends, at arm's length. My core relationships were confusing, although at a cognitive level I knew God gave me a mother to protect, nurture, and mature me.

Mothering is the most significant and demanding profession. We learn our patterns of relating and separating from others from our mother. As children, when our world was a scary and dangerous place, when our emotions were out of control and we had no words to express them, God gave our moms an innate instinct to absorb our fears, worries, sadness, and emotions. God designed us to feel safe and to learn to trust through the caring connection of Mom's arms.

The relational dynamics and patterns that I learned from Mom became the basis of my intimate interactions with others. In my early relationship with my mom, I felt wounded; she was distant, emotionally unavailable, and dismissive of my emotions. In fact, she even determined that I was born with a delicate, emotional constitution, which reflected *weakness*. Mom seldom validated my feelings. When she did not respond with empathy or understanding, I shut down my emotions with criticism, judgment, and self-mockery. I adopted familiar and unhealthy patterns of relating in core relationships by resorting to avoidance, extreme compliance, passivity, and being unable to trust. I internalized those dysfunctional patterns and lived by them. I began to hide my needs and emotions and resist vulnerability. I lost all confidentiality and trust in Mom, becoming defensive, reactive, and ultimately avoidant, burying my emotions. As you can see, these early imprints from Mom developed in my neurobiology, determining how I would operate in other relationships in the future. I realized I was repeating these patterns even as an adult.

We are only capable of passing on or giving what we have received.

⌒

The human brain's highways (neurological pathways) are created for connection by age two. Our brain is about three pounds in weight.[5] It makes up only 2 percent of our body mass, but it uses up to 20 percent of the oxygen and calories we consume on a daily basis. The brain is a very delicate organ made up of about 80 percent water, with the consistency of Jello at room temperature. Our brain is the most complex organ in God's creation. It contains over one hundred billion neurons (nerve cells.)[6] Without counting the supporting glial cells, this is approximately the number of stars in our Milky Way galaxy. Isn't that incredible? Each of those individual neurons has an upward connection that amounts to 10,000 connections with other neurons, which means that our brains have more neurological connections than there are stars in our entire universe. What an amazing Creator!

Even more intriguing is the way individual neurons communicate with each other. The signal initially travels down the length of the neuron electrically. Then the neuron sends a chemical signal across the gap between itself and the adjoining neuron. The neurons don't even touch each other. Scientists have identified over fifteen different types of neurotransmitters—brain chemicals between the individual neurons—and they have begun to study the brain at this level.[7] The millions of unique signals that are sent across the synapse of a single neuron with the various permutations and combinations of the new transmitters are being studied. We think of the computer as complex and sophisticated, but it is so primitive in comparison to the brain. What wires together fires together. Let's take a tour of this battlefield of our mind.

At birth, the human brain is not fully programmed, which is one of its great strengths, as it is infinitely adaptable. The brain isn't completely developed until our mid-twenties, specifically our prefrontal* cortex.[8] The first five years of growth in our brain is critical. Our brains are deeply social organisms for approxi-

---

*. *The prefrontal cortex is the arena of our working memory and concentration. This is also where executive planning, social awareness, and impulse control take place. This is primarily our thinking part of the brain responsible for us making judgments.*

mately 6 to 18 months of age: the right side of our brain is rapidly developing. It is interesting to note that approximately 70 percent of the time, mom carries her infant in her left arm, this is so she can access the right side of the child's brain. The constant interchange of comfort and care that occurs between an emotionally healthy mother and her child is a wonderful and fascinating thing. A mom's healthy interaction works as scaffolding for the construction of the child's social and emotional brain. As a result, the child grows into a young person who can manage and control the negative emotions of life. This also means that if there is abandonment—lack of care between the mother and child—the brain can be set up for some profound struggles.[9]

The first five years of growth in our brains are very critical. Early childhood trauma in the form of abuse or neglect affects the functioning of the brain in ways that negatively impact all stages of social, emotional, and intellectual development.[10] In the first three years of life, as a child is exploring the world by reading, playing, seeing, touching, and feeling, the results are that the neurons are making new connections like crazy. The child's little brain is experiencing everything for the first time, and it is so exciting. This is very different from a fifteen- or seventeen-year-old brain in that there is an extreme difference in the neurological connection.[11] We all develop new neurological freeways in our brain. Instead of thinking all over the place like a three-year-old, we eventually develop fixed ways of thinking, and our neural connections become pruned. Some of the connections we made at three have atrophied and withered because of the lack of use.

So why are we talking about all of these connections? Because our later neurological highways in life come from early construction! Which also means our families of origin taught us how to think and feel in a positive or negative way. These patterns of how we think, based on what we experienced in our homes, also influences our reactions to future pain or trauma.

Needless to say, we really don't leave home, we take it with us—brains and all. In spiritual terms, this can be called a generational curse, ancestral wounds, or transgenerational trauma. Our histories can affect us (our identity) significantly in the present. This is not to say that we aren't responsible for our behaviors in the present because of our past. In the present, if we understand how our past has impacted us (even down to a neurobiological level), we can move to new beginnings.

With this understanding, I decided I needed to reclaim and redeem my past. Moms and dads may have done the best they could, considering the families in which they were raised, but the generational curse can stop when people deal with their childhood traumas and face the pain within.

⁓

Reflection Questions

Have you ever felt you were not worthy of connection with others, not approachable, or unworthy of other's delight in you?

Have you felt isolated or stuck in relationships where you identified something was missing but couldn't put a finger on it?

Did you know that our emotional brains can carry trauma from our infancy, even before we learned to talk?

᷉

Words of encouragement

Let's visit the creation story in the Bible in the first Book of Genesis 1:26-28.[12] *God made Eve a suitable helper for Adam as a helpmate and companion for connection and intimacy because Adam was* **alone***. No human being was created to function or exist in isolation. God created Adam and bestowed him with authority over his creation on the earth. He commanded him to subdue the earth. Scripture tells us that God walked with him by the cool of the day and talked to him daily. Everything was in harmony and synchrony. Yet, God saw Adam was* **lonely***. He needed a companion, someone to fellowship with, pursue, and be close to. God was all sufficient. He was* **good** *and good enough for Adam. But Adam was created by God in his image and he deeply reflected the need for deep fellowship and relationship with him. When God said "a man would leave and cleave," he was making a relational statement before he was making a marriage statement. The God of the Universe created us with a brain that was wired for connection and intimacy for partnership and community. Friends, we are not called to endure our pain in isolation.*

We may have isolated ourselves from others, community, and even God for self-protection, because we were afraid to get hurt, rejected, and abandoned. We were surviving our

115

traumas. When we become aware of our coping mechanisms, like numbing our emotions, perfectionism, performance, etc., and reach out to healthy, mature adults who have walked this journey ahead of us, we have won half our battles. Find a counselor, a trusted friend, or a community that can hold space with you in your burdens and come alongside and walk with you. When we feel overwhelmed with our pain, we need the safety of people who will move willingly into our deep places of woundedness with empathy, compassion, and no judgment. Once we become comfortable expressing our needs and emotions, we will experience comfort and a taste of freedom in our souls.

Final Note

Take heart! There is hope. But we have a choice to break the silence and reach out for help. We don't need to bear these burdens from relational traumas alone. I carried my baggage and wounds into every relationship, including my marriage. It doesn't have to be that way any longer. If you're still breathing, you have hope and the opportunity for redemption and freedom in your soul.

Chapter 8

⁓

The Power of Touch

*"One of the luckiest things that can happen to
you in life is, I think, to have a happy childhood."*
—Agatha Christie

D o you remember the times when you were a little child
and had a problem? Your troubles melted away when
someone you trusted held you close or just gave you a big bear
hug. When children come to us with a boo-boo, their woes dis-
appear as we touch it, kiss it, and put a Band-Aid over it. Safe
touch is crucial to our development as individuals. The opposite
also holds true; I share personal stories here to show you how
the lack of appropriate touch can affect someone.

⁓

I was about three years old and we were saying our goodbyes
as we left my mom's parents' home. "Go give Grandma Eli a

hug," I heard Mom insist again. I was asked to give all the family members a hug. In fact, I was forced to hug them. I detested those hugs and kisses on my face (a combination of an ingested snort and saliva that landed on your cheeks). My Grandma Eli ran over to me and planted a slobbery kiss on my cheek. I remember crystal clear how I took the palm of my left hand and dispelled the wet slime off my face. I was laughed at, made fun of, and reprimanded by Mom and my aunts for my disrespectful act. I was forced to give every person in the household a hug; my mother's sisters, her brothers, and my grandparents.

To this day, I remember the feeling that came over me every time I heard the familiar sentiment, "Something is terribly wrong with you! You must be emotionally damaged with psychological problems." This might have been partially true, but what Mom didn't realize was that she and the others standing around her were a huge part of the problem.

We require healthy physical expressions of affection to acquire normal emotional development. Throughout my growing up years, I was mortified when uncles or grandparents asked me to sit on their laps. Without fail, I would tense my body, mentally shut down, and want to escape. God created us with an innate need for connection, both verbally and through healthy physical contact such as hugging and holding hands with our parents and other significant adult figures in our early years of growth.

An article from Science Daily highlights a study on infant development—how babies' brains process touch and how that builds a foundation for cognitive development skills of imitation, empathy, and connection.[13] We know touch is the first of the five senses to develop, yet scientists are still investigating how a baby's brain responds differently to touch than to say the sight of mom's face or the sound of her voice. Psychologist Andrew Meltzoff states, "Long before babies acquire spoken language, touch is a crucial channel of communication between caregivers and babies."

Scientists have found the following interesting evidence in babies as young as seven months of age about the way they process the sense of touch. The same areas of the brain's neural networks that were activated when babies were touched on the hand or the foot were the same areas that lit up when they saw someone else being touched (observed touch) in the absence of being touched themselves.

As parents, we know, babies watch and imitate what adults do. Imitation is a powerful learning tool for infants. Scientist Melzoff also explains that before babies have words, the recognition that another person is "like me" may be one of the first social insights babies have, and the development of this like-me recognition eventually flowers into feelings of empathy for someone else. Even brain science says the power of touch helps lay the groundwork for the development of cognitive skills; of imitation and empathy, even before we can talk!

Two thousand years ago, the God of the Universe experienced the human power of touch as he was wrapped in the loving arms of a peasant girl from Galilea. He experienced tangible human touch!

There is power in safe touch. God intended for us to receive safe touch from our families in order for us to develop normally in this life.

As we read, even science has found evidence that touch plays a crucial role in the development of empathy-compassion.

Touch was scary, actually mortifying for me. I experienced a huge void, a deficiency of "normal touch" that is present in all healthy family systems. I was anxious around people and experienced a lot of unhealthy and unsafe touch at a very young age, which created dysfunction in my soul: fear, anxiety, worry, insecurity, and relational problems, even into my adult life. Because of these issues, I developed a heightened sense of awareness in my brain—hypervigilance all the time. This even impacted my relationship with my husband and my marriage in general.

At a heart level, I found myself frozen in time even with my own daughter, not wanting to freely hug my child. Whether she came to me at her best or her worst, I would feel my muscles tense when she would reach out to hug me. And yet, I still had to comfort her and nurture her. What a paradox! My traumas of abuse and neglect resided in my body. Secrecy and shame took over—my body, mind, and soul keeping score. The secrecy fed the shame. I didn't have words for those forbidden experiences. They were tucked down deep in the recesses of my soul. Isolation, fear, insecurity, and threat of danger kept me in bondage. It was as if I saw myself, the little wounded girl, in my daughter. And I hated that "inner child" in me.

I was constantly assessing impending danger. I was on high alert all the time. One of the most powerful and healing biological instincts is to hold our babies. It is a basic and natural part of parenting. On the other hand, a lack of touch and parental care can arrest development in key areas. The areas that I lacked development in were the very areas I needed to access to make sure my daughter didn't experience the same childhood that I did, thereby perpetuating the cycle.

I did not share my heart with anyone. If I did, I felt that I was betraying my family. There was a certain loyalty to the family of origin I was trying to preserve. But really, the person I was betraying the most was myself. I had to learn to intentionally do this with both of my children by first learning it for myself. I had to let others nurture and care for me, I had to let other safe women into my life and learn to hug and be hugged freely with no strings attached.

∽

Reflection Questions

Are you willing to ask for what you didn't receive as a child? You need to be willing to ask in a safe place and in a safe community?

Do you think, as I did for three decades, that we don't need to be dependent on others to meet our inner needs?

∽

Words of encouragement

I began to understand that God intended for me to have my basic human needs met. And he intended for me to have these needs met in a healthy manner — to touch and be touched, to be seen, heard, and believed in healthy, loving, and nurturing relationships.

There was something about comfort I had yet to learn. I always felt that I needed to perform to feel worthy of someone's approval or validation. Or I had to take on perfectionism, keeping my environment "in order" to feel a sense of control. I was yet to be touched in my soul — soothed, healed, comforted in every sense. We must learn to ask others who are emotionally healthy and safe if they will meet us in our needs, in our gaps. Find people who will hold us accountable to ensure that we are seeking enough help and not being too dependent.

With the help of my safe "moms"—the women in my life who challenged me, held me accountable, trained me to ask for help, and encouraged me to **receive** their validation and support—I began to grow as an individual. I still had "unfinished business" with Mom and wounds to heal from, but I had a good start. It is most definitely a process and a journey. You need to stick with it; it is not easy, but you will get there with the right support.

∽

Final Note

Jesus touched. Jesus healed people not just in their physical bodies, but also in their souls, in real time. Jesus comforted people tangibly with His presence. There are people around you that God put in your life, in community, who can hold space with you in your wounding. Identify them. Rely on them. We are not called to face our pain alone. Let yourself be healed by their love and support.

Chapter 9

⁓

UNHEALTHY FAMILY

"Feelings of worth can flourish only in an atmosphere where individual differences are appreciated, mistakes are tolerated, communication is open, and rules are flexible – the kind of atmosphere that is found in a nurturing family."

—Virginia Satir

"Behind the mask of indifference is bottomless misery and behind apparent callousness, despair."

—John Bowlby

In this chapter, I will walk you through my "aha" moment when I realized I had an unhealthy family. For years, I was blinded by wishful thinking and fantasy bonding. When all you know is unhealthy bonding, it is hard to identify what is normal and what isn't. This chapter is not about throwing one of my mothering figures (my aunt) under the bus, but rather it is an attempt to "show you" how and when I identified glimpses of the dysfunction in my family.

࿔

It was Christmas 1994, during my undergraduate program. I was living in a hostel run by nuns. We could leave once a month for a visit to our local guardian (my Aunt Sissy and her husband Joe were my guardians at the time). My parents were visiting for two weeks from Africa, and they were planning to stay at Aunt Sissy's. My midterm exams were fast approaching, and my parents would arrive the night of my final paper. I had planned a month ahead and told my warden (matron) about leaving for the weekend to go see my parents right before Christmas break.

My aunt is a Type A planner, so she decided to take her family shopping, and I accompanied them on the shopping spree during my November "guardian visit."

Aunt Sissy had quite a mean demeanor toward me. With a critical spirit, she picked on the way I looked, talked, walked, ate, and even slept. Yes, she even nit-picked me for the way I curled up in the fetal position to sleep when I stayed over at her house during weekend visits. But on this particular day, she commented on my lack of excitement about seeing my parents, who were planning on visiting her soon. She hammered home *all* the sacrifices my mom made for me, including sending me to school in the city to secure a good degree. She went on and on about my character, how emotionless I was, equating me to a rock, and informed me that she was going to help crack the

128

"hard nut" (me).

The barrage continued as we drove through the city. Instead of seeing the beautiful Christmas lights adorning the buildings and street corners, we walked the stores looking for gifts. I couldn't have cared less about the obligatory gift that she was trying to find for me. I was getting exasperated by the attacks on my relationship with my parents—in particular, my mom. I couldn't get these ruminating thoughts and words I had for her out of my head. This was the standard of "beauty" Mom had compared me with at birth? I was reminded in that instance of her words that I had turned dark (and ugly) pretty quickly. Right then, I had my aha moment... Aunt Sissy took my place in my mother's daughter space. And here she was character assassinating me by pulling apart my growing-up years!

With blazing red eyes and a fury that welled up in me, I instantly snapped. "What do you know about my childhood and my relationship with my mom? Why do you feel the need to slam me over this dysfunctional relationship? Who are you to tell me anything about my relationship with my parents without being willing to see past your sister (my mom) as a victim of her children? Do not bring this relationship or this topic up ever again in front of me." I added, "I don't need a gift from you that means nothing to you or to me."

The unbridled me finally unleashed on her. I felt relief, then guilt over what had just happened. She was in tears. God, what did I just do? Did I sin in my fury of disrespect? Was I trying to establish boundaries? My aunt left me alone for the next six months under her guardianship until I finished my undergraduate program.

Despite all this, it was still Aunt Sissy who dropped me off to college for my master's program. She looked proud and surprised when I informed her about my admission based on merit. One billion people in the nation, nineteen open seats, and I made it in. This was nothing short of a miracle. I was glad to be relieved of her guardianship as my next university was four hours away from where she lived.

It was clear to me that Aunt Sissy was doing this "guardian" job for my mother. I figured if she valued me as an individual, she would not have treated me the way she did. In my mind, Mom was here first and it was her responsibility to set the stage for healthy relationships in the extended family. From what I could tell, Aunt Sissy obviously felt she had permission to treat me however she wanted. I was ready to own my part as an adult, but I would not continue permitting my aunt, or anyone else for that matter, to blame me solely for the rupture in this mother-daughter relationship.

When I was a child, I thought like a child. But as an adult, I had to separate from my childhood state and take responsibility for owning up to the hurt and wounding of the past from these mothering figures.

Part of that process was to understand what a healthy family was and what constituted a dysfunctional family.

Two decades later, I received a call from my Aunt Sissy. During the conversation, she brought up my dad, her brother-in-law, who is much older than her. I heard my mom's words through her, "Your father is just lazy! He is like a baby, he doesn't pay attention to what is on the floor; he trips and falls." By this time, Daddy had a diagnosis of Parkinsonism and was developing a fast-growing brain tumor that would totally paralyze him within weeks and eventually take his life. (I lost my father during the last leg of this book project.) I was filled with anger, wanting to stand up and advocate for my disabled dad who was deteriorating quickly and losing his ability to walk, talk, and swallow. I so wanted to retort with a response that would shut her up for this verbal insult. Instead, I maintained my calm and told her to counsel Mom away from talking down to my father due to his developing disability. I suggested she was the right person because she was a Rehabilitation Nurse for an inpatient rehab hospital and often interacted with patients and families with similar disabilities. She could make the most sense to her sister, my mom, who is a trained Christian Counselor. (Personally, I believe Mom should have been in counseling for personal healing for her brokenness in life, her own insecurities and abandonment issues, and her marriage instead of training to become a counselor.)

My aunt, at the end of the conversation, told me that my family *wasn't* dysfunctional and that I *shouldn't* ever once have that thought! She concluded our conversation by saying that I was very articulate in the way I communicated, that my words were mature. However, she would be on Mom's team! Wrong conclusion, right?!? That was dysfunction to the T. At that moment, I realized just how dysfunctional my aunt and my family were.

Codependency loses all sight of reason, common sense, and average intelligence. It's as if all mental faculties quickly go out the window when codependency is present. My mother was in the role of victim. Her sisters, especially my Aunt Sissy, was feeding her codependent energy, encouraging her, and participating in slander and a gang-up mentality. After that conversation, my eyes were widely opened as to what a dysfunctional family really was. Thankfully, with help from my therapists and recovery groups, I learned more about dysfunctional families and could see how this dysfunction occurred in my own family.

Dysfunctional family: a family in which some behavior such as alcoholism, drug abuse, divorce, an absent father or mother, excessive anger, verbal or physical abuse interferes with the ability of the family to do its job effectively.

How well we survive childhood traumas of abandonment, neglect, and abuse will depend on how well the family has learned to function together. "Dysfunctional" is used to express the inability of family members to meet the God-given needs and functions in a family. These families are unable to communicate their feelings, both positively and negatively, in a caring and consistent way. Family members are unable to respond to the needs of each other within the family unit. Period.

I was forced to think about what each family member individually represented to me. I journaled words that came to my mind. When I thought about the word "mom" it surely *did not* represent comfort, nurture, or compassion. For me, I associated the word "mom" with neglect, emotional absence, lack of value, and a dislike for me. I sensed a level of jealousy and a level of "you don't deserve this life you're living" mentality. Feelings that were brought up for me were anger, bitterness, lack of feeling valued, loved, or cherished, and I am not so proud to say that. For me, I had many mothering figures. My paternal aunt represented nurture, concern, playfulness, and my feelings toward her were love and trust. My grandmother (Sara) on my paternal side represented nurture, protection, empathy, and concern.

My eyes were opened the day I realized my family, unfortunately, fell into this category of a dysfunctional family.

Let's take a look at the characteristics of a dysfunctional family.

Needy family member:

The energy and attention of the family are directed toward caring for the needs of the emotions of this one family member. Then, all the family members become emotionally needy. In a dysfunctional family, the family members operate according to spoken or unspoken rules and not necessarily according to personal needs or needs being met.

My mom always demonstrated negative energy, making others responsible for her needs, especially her emotional needs.

Denial and secrecy:

Problems and conflict are part of any family. Healthy families have problems, expect problems, and have healthy ways of coping with them. Members of the family talk about and through issues, even though someone may feel embarrassed or hurt. Family members take responsibility for their own behaviors, and problems are discussed with solutions in mind. In dysfunctional families, the "don't talk" rule keeps the offended party in bondage.

Repressed emotions, explosive emotions, or both:

In a healthy family, emotions are modeled, permitted, and expressed. Children learn how to identify and deal with their feelings. In a dysfunctional family, all emotions are forbidden.

I was a very sensitive child who discerned intuitively and empathetically felt others' emotions, yet I learned not to show much emotion. When I cried, I was compared to an aunt by my mother, and she laughed or ridiculed me for this. Often times I was told, "something was inherently wrong with me." And then I was told it was a joke. Haha… what a joke!

In reality, I was being told, or given, the messages, "Don't express your feelings," "You don't have permission to cry or get angry," "Don't betray the family," "Don't you ever dare tell someone outside this family about inside stories." These messages were absolutely detrimental and created in me this belief system that took root in my brain—that's right, in my emotional brain and primitive brain, more specifically my limbic system— that I could not feel my emotions.

⟡

Reflection Questions

Have you been told you're not good enough, or smart enough, or that you had to work so hard to make it in this life?

We can all feel like a failure or be shamed with any number of derogatory or belittling statements. All of these are characteristics of family systems, and are based on shame and dysfunction.

⟡

Words of encouragement

In God's family system, we were not created to feel shame. Remember the story of Adam and Eve in the garden. The original family went into dysfunction, which resulted in the fall. By default, all of us were born into dysfunctional families to varying degrees, but we can heal and be restored by the recovery skills that are available to us in God's word and his blueprint for a family: secure attachment. Seek counseling or recovery groups that specifically deal with dysfunctional family dynamics, and healing from those dynamics will be real and possible.

Conclusion to Part II - Created on Purpose

W*e were created on purpose, hard-wired for connection—to connect authentically with another human being and to connect deeply with others in community.
Even when unpredictable things happen in our lives in this
fallen world, we can build resilience in authentic and safe
connections. When God created Adam, he made a relational
connection with him before his marriage connection with
Eve. God was perfectly sufficient for Adam for companion-
ship, everything was good and going well in the garden.
But he saw Adam was alone, practically lonely. And so, he
provided another human being for him: Eve. You and I did
not arrive into this world as fully-grown women and men.
If we belong to humankind, it took us the womb of a woman,
our mother, to arrive in this world. We simply cannot argue
against that. We were created as infants to be completely
dependent on another human being. That is the way it is
supposed to be. No job can compete with the significance of
a mother's heart to mold her child in this life.*

*We are told in scripture that children are a "blessing."
They are a loving gift, worthy of our admiration and respect!
As Billy Graham wisely said, "Only God Himself fully ap-
preciates the influence of a Christian mother in the molding
of character in her children." As Henry Ward Beecher says,*

"The Mother's heart is a child's schoolroom." I realized that my mother was only capable of passing down what she received in her attachment history. She was passing down intergenerational trauma.

I simply chose to recognize those things that needed repair so I could redeem my purpose. I recognized that I carried a brokenness in my soul from the wounds Mom inflicted upon me from her dysfunctional and wounded attachment history. I've written about my disintegrated self, which I was trying to identify in my young adulthood, in the next section of this book.

PART III:

∿

BROKEN IDENTITY

Introduction to Part III

*T*he pain caused by emotional and spiritual wounds due to neglect and abandonment in my life needed to be released. The voices that I heard in my early years created a belief system that took deep root in my personhood as a child, growing stronger into my adulthood. We all respond to damage caused by childhood wounding in varying degrees. Regardless of how significantly we were affected, we need to face the damage it caused. I certainly wasn't immune or scar-free, even into my adulthood.

Writing about what was unjust in my story gave me freedom from the tentacles of those who kept me in the prison of my own mind for over four decades. There is nothing faker than living a life on replay, trapped by childhood trauma. In this section, I will walk you through how those patterns and lies took deep root in my core, my personhood, and my essence.

Author's Note: My intent in these next several chapters, is not to mom-bash or throw moms and mothering figures under the bus. It is only my attempt to explain how trauma within the mother-child relationship can affect us throughout our lives. I have stripped my soul naked as a result.

Chapter 10

༄

LIES MAGNIFIED – WHO AM I?

*"In the social jungle of human exis-
tence, there is no feeling of being alive
without a sense of identity."*
—Erik Erikson

*"Unlike a drop of water which loses its
identity when it joins the ocean, man does
not lose his being in the society in which
he lives. Man's life is independent. He is
born not for the development of the society
alone, but for the development of his self."*
—B.R, Ambedkar

T he attachment figures—my mother and other family
members—who were a part of my early life were sup-

posed to nurture, cherish, and create a sense of self-worth in me. Instead, they failed miserably, creating many challenges in my life going forward. They were here on this earth before me and thus responsible for how our relationship began. Most of these relationships yielded me many years of feeling abandoned and neglected. In this chapter, I will walk you through how my childhood patterns of dysfunctionality and my broken identity began to define who I was as an adult.

⟂

During my early adult years, I felt like my life—my core—had lost its identity in the ocean of my upside-down relational patterns. Mom had just graduated with a master's degree in counseling when I visited Botswana after leaving my first dream job at the Institute for Cognitive and Communicative Neurosciences (in India). I was putting all my energy and efforts into my work as a consultant speech-language pathologist who worked on a United Nations developmental project in the area of learning disabilities, the first of its kind in the nation at the time. I knew I was called to this job, yet I felt compelled to leave it, and all its perks, to care for my mom post-surgery for six months. Caretaking was a role I was so easily entangled with. I was coaxed into thinking and believing that this was my responsibility. I also fell for the bait that there were bigger possibilities for finding a better job in Botswana. The grass is always greener on the other side, right?

I volunteered during the week at the only hospital in Botswana that offered Speech-Language Pathology and Audiology services at the time. The department head happened to be from my alma mater. I learned a great deal under his leadership as a volunteer intern in the department.

On the weekends, I accompanied Mom to work where I would volunteer my time talking to the young adults she worked with. She provided counseling services on AIDS prevention and how to emotionally deal and live with the disease. The need was great in Botswana, being the world's largest AIDS-stricken country at the time.

During weeknights, after I got home from my volunteer work, my ears were frequently bombarded with a litany of verbal insults. To date, I am convinced Mom believed she was advising me. Living with her, the fight began yet again. Once more (this time at the age of twenty-four) I heard: "You're getting too old, you need to marry." "You're of age, delaying your marriage any later than now will result in infertility," —this one Mother reminded me of frequently. I was labeled too sensitive, too anxious, a hard nut to crack, and trapped in my emotions without a future ahead. As the oldest child, I internalized that the family problems were mine to own and fix. If I didn't fulfill the expectations of rescuing everybody from their life circumstances, bad choices, or status quo situations, then I became the black sheep of the family.

I simply could not meet these unrealistic expectations that were placed on me. When I did stand up for myself and against verbal attacks, I was labeled as having "a sickness in my bones." I was told that I had an anger problem; I took words too seriously, had a deficient sense of humor, and was advised to receive and treat them as a joke. And the crazy loop began again. I had ruminating thoughts of wanting to get back at Mom—the verbal tapes played on repeat in my head!

I felt like a ragged doll in a puppet show who was getting tired and slowly building up a volcano on the inside, ready to explode any time. The six months I spent volunteering my time and living with Mom was also one of the most isolating, depressing times of my entire life—enduring manipulation and control for months. I believe my mom didn't experience or know a better way. I quickly realized the trap I was in. My parents lived apart from each other—Mom lived in the capital city of Gaborone, Botswana and my father lived in a small village town fifty kilometers away. They paid rent for two different houses. Dad visited us in the apartment on the weekends. In addition to the constant bickering, fighting, yelling, and screaming that occurred in the home when they were together, they began begging, bantering, and utilizing force to convince me of the arranged marriage proposals that were frequently brought forward.

I believe at their core my parents wanted to see me married soon, as I was old by cultural standards. My state of singleness was posing the threat for them to be harassed and ridiculed in the local culture and community as well. In turn, they continued pestering me to consider marriage alliances. I certainly felt guilty that they were prey to social disgrace because of me.

"Your dad is going to have a heart attack pretty soon," my mother said.

"How do you know that?" I asked.

"Well, the amount of stress you are putting him through every time you say 'No' to a marriage proposal is enough to cause him a heart attack!"

"Dad and Mom, how about Jojo who resides in the Cape of Good Hope in South Africa? I think I like him," I said.

"Oh, no way! His mother is on antidepressants, you know. And these things certainly run in the family," Mom declared. With her counseling background, I wasn't going to argue with her about this point. I asked about Milan, whose parents had just made contact with them. "He is an engineer—that's good, but his father has a plantain farm and sells bananas at the local market!" said Mom.

My mom then went on to read another arranged marriage profile from an email she had recently received. That was it for me. I announced a big fat "No" to anyone else my mom brought up. My parents viciously fought with each other. From that time forward, they consistently declined marriage proposals, even the ones I was willing to consider, and labeled them as not *fit* for me. I slid back into my familiar pattern. I snapped, telling them that I wanted nothing to do with one more alliance if marriage was what *they* modeled.

At that very moment, it felt like hell had just transcended down into the apartment. My mother called me every name in the book. When I stood up to her, she cursed my father's family and told me, "Don't you dare speak to me like that ever again!"

I emphatically said "No" to marriage. My head felt faint, my body began shaking. I could barely see through my foggy eyes, tears welling up, darkness beginning to squelch me. The scornful words spoken suffocated me. This dynamic of manipulation and emotional blackmail was all too familiar.

I felt the anger building up like a volcano, erupting out of my nostrils like fumes of smoke. My breath felt warm on my upper lips. The hairs on my nape stood up as I vomited this verbal diarrhea, "Mom, I have endured enough of your *verbal abuse* for a quarter of a century." Mother was taken aback as much I was by my determined tone of voice when I finally found the words to stand up to her and name it as "verbal abuse." Mom then blamed my genes for my behavior. I explained that I had fifty percent of her DNA and fifty percent of dad's, and my speaking voice that she had just witnessed was hers and dad's voices put together!

After this cathartic episode, the world around me felt calm— but only for a moment. Before I knew it, though, I quickly slid back into my childhood state of feeling small, minuscule, insignificant, unseen, and unheard, just like when I was a little girl. I became the puny, frightened child I was at age five. *Nothing had changed*.

I cried, begging her to find me a ticket and put me on an airplane back to India. I was done with "survival" in this environment. My stomach developed ulcers. I lost weight as my stomach regurgitated every morsel of food I placed on my tongue. I looked at myself one morning in the mirror; I finally *saw* my bones sticking out of my elbows at my arms. My sunken face, with heavy eyelids and black circles around my eyes, gazed back at me with contemplation and trepidation at the current state of my life. I looked like a living skeleton. I needed to leave, and it had to be soon. *My survival instincts wanted me to be on the run again!*

Living in an apartment under the same roof with Mom for half of that year was the most burdensome and exhausting time of my life—who would believe this story if I were to tell anyone? How would I find anyone who would be willing to lend a listening ear? I continued reliving the lies that I heard day in and day out as a child. My lies magnified. The bells of those lies rang strongly in my head—"I was good for nothing." Friends,

146

neighbors, and extended family members gave me a diagnosis of clinical depression. I agree that must have been true. My only respite was the time I was serving people and volunteering at the hospital. It brought a wellspring of life and joy into my soul. This joy was short-lived, but it was at least something—a feeling, a memory I could hang on to and draw from.

In contrast, every single time I stepped one foot back into the apartment, those lies magnified like a trumpet blaring loudly in my brain and playing on repeat. Every night I ruminated on the words Mom spoke to me that day, only to keep me awake all night. I waited for the first rays of sunlight to signal me from my waking slumber so I could meet "joy" again at my volunteering job. I did not have enough money on my own to buy a plane ticket to leave. I was a grown adult at twenty-four years of age, living with my mother in an apartment, tired of the verbal and emotional insults given in the name of "parenting" and under the guise of "teaching and guidance."

Living with Mom as an adult felt like a repeat of the life I had lived as a young child.

ᘒ

Finally, after begging my parents to send me back to India, they did purchase a flight to send me back home! I was happy to return to my Grandma Sara's since I anticipated leaving India soon. I had several job interviews from the States that were promising.

One of those job opportunities panned out, and I left two continents behind and moved to the United States for a new job. I was still on the run to find home, security, and stability. But the "voices" of my mother still had power over me, haunting, guilt-tripping, and emotionally manipulating me. Fear had a stranglehold on me, and I felt imprisoned.

Restless and emotionally tired with my chronic insomnia and caffeine-addicted brain (immune to the effects of twelve large cups of coffee a day), I learned to survive my new workday with its new environment and country. But despite this, my broken identity continually screamed loud in my head, and I wasn't quite sure of whom I had become anymore. My identity seemed to be wrapped up in whom everyone else said I was or *what* I was good at. My whole world was filled with projects.

I continued to work to fulfill the expectations my family had of me, both spoken and unspoken. I was to be the rescuer of the immediate family. If I didn't rescue them from their emotions, feelings, circumstances, or financial situation, I went on a guilt trip. I had let others set up false expectations for myself that became the mantra of my family system, which was spread across the globe. I felt obligated to a family who was conditional in their interactions. If I met their expectations and continued to be a scapegoat to fulfill their demands and wishes, then I was lovable; if not, I was evil, for lack of a better word.

Soon, my mom was back in the swing of her vicious cycle, running her daily anxiety and worries about how I would marry and start a family so late in life, even though I was only twenty-four at the time. Again and again, she reminded me that I would have trouble bearing children or I would give birth to children with disabilities due to late pregnancies. This was the main driving goal of her daily phone conversations with me. My mom constantly asked if I was waiting to have teeth sticking out through my nose or dentures hanging out of my mouth before I started thinking about getting married. I broke the rules; I simply did not receive this as a joke or think this was a funny statement.

Little did I realize this was a vortex of craziness, as I was being controlled, manipulated, and emotionally blackmailed as a grown adult, I went back to my three-year-old self, trapped, helpless and emotionally shut down. What was wrong with me? Why was I behaving this way?

Several years later, I was totally set up for a plethora of lies that had grown deep roots in my soul, body, and spirit. My body, my will, my mind, and my emotions were fogged by these lies. I thank God for my midlife awakening. Almost four decades later, I finally decided to see a therapist. Initially, we had to work through my childhood trauma, addressing my parental attachment dysfunction issues—my deep mother-wounds.

"An emotionally abused woman," my therapist said.

"Who is that?" I asked.

Who was I?

It finally sounded like there was an answer to the questions I had asked myself for several decades of my life. My therapist named the answer: *"You have been emotionally abused. Because it has been over such a long period of time, your brain doesn't even recognize it!"*

I had been through all different kinds of abuse, but this one in particular—emotional abuse from my mom and mothering figures—was what I was dealing with at the core of my being.

I am an emotionally abused woman!

Ha! What a statement; what a terrible thing to own. My therapist had to work hard to convince me that such a thing existed in my life. How could Mom(s) emotionally abuse me? The very people I loved, and of course whom I believed loved and cared about me, could not have abused me. Right? I had to come to terms with my denial and fantasy relationship with my family, especially my mom.

Because I had a long and established pattern of continually being abused by those I was involved with, no matter how successful, intelligent or attractive others told me I was, I still felt "less than." I had trouble standing up for myself in relationships in my adult life; with bosses, friends, parent(s), other parental figures, aunts, uncles, siblings, and sometimes even with my own children. No matter how hard I tried, I was victimized by my low self-esteem. I was fearful of authority figures. I was living with the effects of emotional abuse and I had no idea. I was suffering from its effects: depression, lack of motivation, difficulty concentrating, insomnia, low self-esteem, worthlessness, feelings of failure, self-blame, self-destructiveness. Most of all, I didn't own the life I was living, including all of the talents, potential, and capabilities I possessed.

I was educated; I had dual undergraduate and master's degrees; I had worked in leadership and administrative positions; I did my jobs well; I had excellent performance reviews and annual reports; and yet I failed to believe in myself or in my achievements. I felt like I was living outside of myself, watching this other individual go on a roller coaster ride—in and out, up and down she went, spiraling out of control into the dark, deep abyss of denial.

What is emotional abuse?

Emotional abuse is any kind of abuse that is emotional in nature; behavior that is designed to control or subjugate another human being through the use of fear. It can include anything from verbal assault, constant criticism to more subtle tactics such as intimidation, manipulation, and fear.[14]

True emotional abuse brainwashes the victim to systematically wear at the core of a person's self-confidence and sense of self-worth, to where he or she develops mistrust in his or her perception or self-concept. Regardless of whether it is done by constant belittling and intimidation or under the guise of "guidance" and "teaching," the results are similar. Eventually, the recipient loses all sense of personal value, creating scars that may be far deeper and more lasting than physical ones. Even with physical and sexual abuse, the greater proportion of damage after the traumatic events that passes on is emotional in nature.

In emotional abuse, the criticisms, the accusations, the insults slowly eat away at the victim's self-esteem until she becomes immune to the situation, incapable of judging it for what it is. Without much realization, she continues to find herself in those patterns of relating over and over again. The ultimate fear of losing the relationship keeps her stuck in the relationship like a child (who doesn't have a good sense of self). Most of the time, the emotionally abused person is victimized by more than one person. This is because the pattern of abuse often starts when the person was a young child, and she or he grows up with low self-esteem and with the expectation of being abused. This attracts other abusers into their life. Through a new lens, I remembered stories that Grandma Eli told me about her life when I visited her for the holidays every year in grade school. And it all began to make sense; emotional abuse had been passed down through the generations! Hurt people were hurting their children and their children's children.

Every holiday, I went to Grandma Eli's house (accompanied by one sibling at times) for a few days. Grandma Eli told me stories of her past, about raising her children, and of her childhood home and her life. Grandma recounted, "I was so young, barely eighteen. I had no idea what to expect when I came to my husband's home as his new bride, but I also didn't know what to expect from my mother-in-law. I was expected to work all the chores inside and outside the home. I fed the cows, cut grass from the field, rolled up the hay, and brought it home to the stable. Soon I became pregnant, sick as a dog, yet there was no mercy."

In addition, to the severe verbal and emotional abuse Grandma Eli endured, she wasn't permitted to serve herself or eat in the kitchen. Tears rolled down her cheeks and she sobbed uncontrollably as she recounted these abuses. She could not hide the tears, although she tried hard. My heart went out to her as she continued to tell me her story. She shared how she waited and ate the last bit of rice from the pot that was mixed with stones, which was the biggest meal of the day while she was pregnant, served by her mother-in-law. Grandma Eli dragged her pregnant belly out into the field again early the next morning before the sun came out. I wondered how my great-grandma treated my grandpa.

She told me that sometimes she ran away from her husband's home and went back to her mother's house. I put two and two together and understood that this is perhaps where my mother learned that going to her mother's house was a safe haven. My mom is the second-born of nine children. Grandma Eli lost two babies. From other stories, I gathered that my older, responsible aunt mothered my mom. I had some empathy visualizing the verbal and emotional abuse that was modeled in the home and that was continually passed down the generations. Some of the patterns of behavior made sense, however, the "gaslighting" my mom displayed would take over any rational conversation I tried to have with her.

I was raised to be compliant, to smooth things over, to be respectful to my parents and elders, and *submit* to them. Mom constantly talked to us about children needing to submit to her, even quoting scriptures! If I dared try to bring up the issue of submission, it became my fault. According to my mom, everything that was relationally wrong with the parent-child relationship was the child's fault. *Always!*

I was *suppressed* in response to the emotional and verbal abuse of many women in my life. The day I realized this pattern of behavior was emotional abuse, I began to identify these behaviors, and I decided I was going to take steps toward my healing. Like me, most who are emotionally abused will have resistance to the idea at first. I continued doubting myself, in fact, even doubting if this was indeed emotional abuse or if I was making a mountain out of a molehill. I was denying something was really wrong, and instead blamed myself, "Something is really wrong with *you*." After all, that is what I consistently heard.

It was very painful to come to terms with the fact that someone I actually loved, and who was supposed to love me in return, was emotionally and psychologically abusing me intentionally or unintentionally.

We might love them too much to give them the benefit of the doubt or find an explanation for their behavior, especially if they are good to us "conditionally" on other occasions.

The following are some of the emotionally abusive behaviors I identified with the help of my therapist.

Emotional abusers are dominating and controlling

Verbal assaults including belittling, criticizing, name-calling, blaming, using sarcasm, and humiliation are intended to damage the recipient's self-esteem and self-image. Emotional abuse involves demeaning someone intentionally: being mean, un-concerning, and even cruel. The key here is that emotional abusers make you feel bad about yourself, and it makes them feel superior to you which gives him or her the feeling of power, and now they can control your emotions, too. You have the right to feel your emotions. No one can tell you how or what you should feel. You are in control of this. Every time you encounter the abuser, they are unrelentingly critical of you, always finding fault, and they can never be pleased.

It is the cumulative effect of the insidious nature of the abuse that does the damage over time. It eats away at your self-confidence and self-worth and undermines any good feelings you have about your accomplishments or achievements, eventually convincing you that nothing you do is worthy or worthwhile, and you may feel like just giving up. Just as much as physical violence assaults the body, verbal and emotional abuse assaults the mind and the spirit, causing deep wounds that are extremely damaging and difficult to heal from. But not impossible. Otherwise, I wouldn't be writing this book!

Emotional abusers place their demands on you with unreasonable and unrealistic expectations

You're expected to drop or put aside everything to satisfy his or her needs (including emotional needs). No matter how much attention, time, or resources you give them, they are never pleased because there is always something more you could have done, or should have done! You are subjected to constant criticism to your face or behind your back. You are constantly berated because you don't fulfill all of their unrealistic expectations at your cost.

Emotional abusers use
blackmail as a tool

This is a very powerful way of manipulating and coercing another person into either consciously or unconsciously doing what they want you to do by playing into your fear and compassion and running you on a guilt trip. For example, I was told that I was causing a lot of emotional distress on my father when I established emotional boundaries with Mom to address the verbal and emotional abuse from her. She always brought my dad who was sick, into the middle of the situation to get her way by guilt-tripping me. I was made to feel guilty if I put my needs or my family's needs, including my daughter's chronic illness, ahead of my mother's emotional needs. When we couldn't travel to India to go visit as a family (because it would put my daughter's life at risk), I was nagged by extended family members on behalf of Mom about how terrible a daughter I was, failing my duty as a daughter.

Unfortunately, this included my younger siblings. Since that's the only model they received, they felt empowered in the art of blaming, gaslighting, emotionally blackmailing, and guilt tripping. My emotional abusers used fear tactics, blaming and guilting to get me under their control, constantly dismissing me as inconsiderate, selfish, or bad. I almost felt guilty for living my own life. It felt like I was undeserving of living this life or putting my own family first.

Emotional blackmailers with their unrealistic expectations often tell you that they didn't mean it that way. When he or she blames you because his or her life is a mess, you are expected to somehow make it better for them. It is not your job to fix their problems, cover their sin, or make their life easier. Each of us is responsible for our own load, our own conduct, and our own feelings. An abuser tries to make you responsible so he or she doesn't have to be. They then try to make you responsible or blame you for not fixing things the way they wanted them fixed! And this is despite you owning up to your part of the problem. Galatians 6:5 says, "For we are each responsible for our loads." Yes, we are to help carry each other's burdens, but each one of us is still responsible (deal with, figure out, fix) for the cross (load) we bear.

Emotional abusers use children to get their way, no matter the cost.

The abuser wants to take the place of God in your life. When children come along, they see you caring for them and will say things like, "You love them more than you love us," trying to make you feel guilty for caring for and loving your own children. My mom always told me that I expended "too much energy" caring for my chronically-ill children, as I made the decision to leave my full-time job, finding part-time work and weekend gigs to make it work. I was told that my children have a terrible model of parenting, and if I didn't correct the way I related to my parents, in particular, my mom, I should expect to be treated the "same way" from my children. I had to learn that boundaries were necessary to establish "separateness" from my mom and to break off from my codependency.

Emotional abusers
will make attempts to
assassinate your character.

This occurs in all different forms, including constantly blowing things out of proportion, gossiping about your mistakes and past failures, humiliating, criticizing, making fun of you in front of others, minimizing you, and discounting your achievements—all in an effort to ruin you personally or professionally. This often causes you lost relationships. They slander you and then deny that they ever made such comments in front of you or behind your back.

Emotional abusers love to sabotage other relationships and want to decide whom you spend time with and whom you talk to. Remember, if the goal of the emotional abuser is to have power and control over you, an abuser doesn't want you to have a support system of people who love you, who love you more than they do, or who can help you escape his/her control. If you have better relationships with your children, then he or she will want to ruin those relationships by triangulating (telling two different people two different stories specifically about the other person to cause a problem in that relationship). In these situations, you must get the support you need to see unhealthy, abusive behaviors for what they are. Abusers control you and the relationship.

Emotional abusers are great at gaslighting.

Gaslighting is a term used to describe when the abuser makes another person doubt her character, her perceptions, her memory, and her own sanity.

Have you ever tried to share your feelings or a problem only to end up feeling like you are crazy for being that way? Believing that if you were less abusive or a better person there wouldn't be a problem in the first place? Have you been thought of as hysterical for even thinking there was an issue to talk about?

This was a repeated occurrence with my mother and my siblings in my young adult and adult life. If you feel blamed each and every time you try to express your feelings or address a problem, this is more than a communication issue. Each of us is entitled to our feelings. We should take the time to listen to each other's feelings, even if those feelings are a result of something we've done. But when the conversation seems to go in circles *after* you've examined your part in a problem and taken ownership, with you being blamed for having feelings, you are being gaslighted.

For example, when I told my mom that I felt angry at her for all the times I was emotionally abused, she said that I had a sickness in my bones and I should not be so silly. Yes, emotional abusers are great at invalidating your feelings because they don't want to acknowledge that you have been emotionally abused. An emotionally abusive person will "forget" or continually deny that something was said. They will deny or exaggerate events by insinuating that you are lying. They convincingly "transfer" their abusive parts to you. By doing these things, the abuser is trying to gain control over you and avoid responsibility for his side of the situation or his action.

Emotional abusers threaten to withhold love and abuse physically.

In this instance, one person is physically overpowering the other, for example, a caretaker physically twisting the arm of a disabled person who is physically immobile when he is trying to communicate a need. Pushing, threatening to beat, shove, and physically exerting force are all red flags that the abuse is escalating and someone is getting hurt. No amount of good behavior on your part is going to stop the need for power from the abuser in this struggle. Often people think if they are not being kicked, punched, or beaten up they are not experiencing domestic violence. In addition to physical violence, abuse can include punching walls, pushing, or standing in your way—anything used to intimidate or insinuate physical harm.

෴

We are all guilty of behaving in some of the ways listed above. Because, let's be honest, in the heat of an argument or in an unhealthy relationship either or both parties might end up criticizing, arguing, and bickering. One or both parties may even resort to name calling. So what, then, qualifies these behaviors as abuse? What is the difference?

If it is *consistent*, meaning every time an individual interacts with you, if it is destructive and consciously intended for you to feel bad and you are devalued as a person, or if there is intent to dominate and control rather than give constructive criticism, then it is emotional abuse. In a healthy relationship, the end goal is always to "repair" versus to "win" in the relationship. The abuser overall has a lack of value, worth, and has a general sense of disrespect for you. It has nothing to do with something specific you are doing or not doing at the moment. It is a *strong pattern* of consistent behavior.

Emotional abusers do not like it when you develop a sense of self and have boundaries. It was a rude awakening when I realized I was in a *codependent* relationship with the people who abused me!

Envy, jealousy, a competitive spirit, and possibly a history of abuse may drive an abuser to stay in the power struggle of control. Many times I thought I was making a big deal about the words of my abuser that were intentionally hurtful. My abusers would tell me that they were just joking or that I was too sensitive or didn't know how to take a joke lightly.

Let me highlight again that emotional abuse can come from dad, mom, siblings, uncles, aunts, friends, co-workers, or even your boss. The emotional abuser is capable of turning around and blaming you for their behavior. The need for them to justify their behavior is also your fault. They will always make you feel like you are deserving of their abuse by consistently diminishing, demeaning, devaluing, and consistently disrespecting you. Emotional abusers are abandoners. They are irresponsible with a lack of ownership for their behaviors.

If you are experiencing physical or emotional abuse, it is time to seek help from a professional or someone trained to help victims of abuse. Do not be a bystander. Both men and women should stand up against any type of abuse toward any human being.

Seek out professional help via a counselor or even a domestic violence agency. These services are not just for people experiencing physical violence. You DON'T need a physical bruise to get help from a domestic violence organization or shelter. (Check the resource list for the hotline number.)

Reflection Questions

Have you ever been emotionally abused by a parent, spouse, uncle, aunt, sibling, or any person with whom you felt unsafe? Have you felt like a child—in a power-down position, with the other person in a power-up situation **consistently***?*

Have you felt that way with a co-worker, boss, or even a friend—someone who you thought was for you? Maybe they made you believe they were for you but then disappeared after they betrayed or slandered you behind your back?

∼✑

Words of encouragement

Have you heard of the story of Paneana, the woman who insulted Hannah, despised her, and scorned her?

Have you heard of the story of Sarah who emotionally abused Hagar out of jealousy? She bore a child for Abraham, a child who was totally not planned in God's will or his idea for her.

If people have used and abused you verbally or otherwise, in particular as a woman, take heart, there are plenty of stories in the Bible. Misogyny existed in ancient times! Yes, in biblical times. How awful, but then a holy, just, and righteous God did not omit these stories out of the Bible. God had a plan for both Hannah and Hagar's lives. At the end of the day, God's plan and promise eventually came to pass even in these crazy circumstances.

~⑨

Final Note

*Don't beat yourself up if you cannot change your behavior of succumbing to emotional abuse or core dysfunctional patterns overnight. It took several years for me to get to a better place. I haven't completely arrived yet either. You have a right to get "angry enough" and "hate" what is unjust in order to move forward and choose **safety**. Be aware of it, and don't reside in anger to a point where it becomes a problem. This is definitely a path and a process. Don't rush to forgive; you have to process the hurt to be able to release it. The cross of Christ is sufficient to be a buffer between you and the abuser. We can release the hurt into the mercy river of God.*

Chapter 11

꩜

A Bit of Canaan

"Adventure must start with running away from home."

—William Bolitho

This chapter talks about my adventures while on the run—to find stability, security, and home. People have been in search of home and wholeness since the beginning—the untouched garden of Eden. I, too, was in search of the promised land, my Canaan!

For years I spent time in a wilderness of isolation, circling the same mountain of my emotions and relational patterns. My primitive (downstairs) brain had learned to overtake my thinking (upstairs) brain. God created our downstairs brain to help us sense danger, which triggers our autonomous nervous systems to respond, taking us away from danger. But I was living with my downstairs brain, which held my emotions including fear, terror, anxiety, and paranoia. You name it, I was triggered by it at the drop of a hat. But most of all, I was on the run, in search of home.

⁓

I had traveled around the globe and come to the United States on my own with a new job. A friend of mine was leaving his job and introduced me to his manager who was looking to immediately hire. Later, when I referred a friend to the interviewer, he reported that horses and mules don't go where I was hired, referring to the very small town in northern Michigan where I was sent!

I still felt like God had answered my prayers in taking me far away from my family, somewhere close to the Arctic. I was in a new place; I had an accent; I felt a little like a misfit all the way around, yet secretly, I rejoiced at the physical distance between myself and my family.

The encapsulated child in me was still on the run from unhealthy and dysfunction. Although the experience of *home* for me was living as a vagabond, with a brain wired by nomadism, unpredictability, and separation from stability and security, I did experience glimpses of *home* in my life's journey across the globe.

I wasn't kidding when I said God took me to the Arctic. Welcome to Canaan—my life in Michigan! I made friends at work, on walks, and at the only grocery store in town. I found a church on the hill that literally became a beacon in my life—a lighthouse. Now, when I say small town, I mean it was really small with a population of about five hundred people. I stayed at an "inn" run by Ms. Shelby. Mr. Eves oversaw the place. The first floor had a small, common kitchen, an electric stove, and was generally empty except for the dishes piled in the sink.

I mostly heated up canned soups or fixed myself something quick like a ham sandwich to avoid the stares from my peculiar "inn mates." They peered at me through hollow, glassy eyes and double frowns. Some looked outside the glass window, staring aimlessly into space. *Who were these downtrodden, lost souls?* I wondered.

As I looked outside the window and saw the snow-covered rooftops of the Tudor-style, fifty-year-old buildings, it reminded me of a postcard. Seeing snowfall for the very first time in my life was thrilling! It appeared that the God of the Universe was dropping soft crystals to the ground. My early morning ritual was to come down and make myself a pot of coffee and then to answer calls from my parents or other family members who lived in North America. I was met with strange, eerie looks from Mr. Eves, a heavy-set man. His long, peering glance from across the hallway through a semi-closed door would catch me off-guard. Was Mr. Eves overhearing my conversations or trying to plan some clandestine act? These were frequent thoughts (triggers) that crossed my mind as I lived in this isolated and strange place.

A few random people sometimes made eye contact or forced out a "Hi." A usual encounter was with an elderly woman who lived downstairs and sat in a rocker, crocheting all day. At times, she broke into a smile as I walked in through the main door from work. Something in the air smelled "creepy" most of the time, and my primitive brain shrieked "unsafe." I thought, *Well, my job put me here after all. It has to be okay.*

I did not have a landline or cell phone. I had to depend on folks calling on the landlord's line. It was a lonely and isolating existence, which was only interrupted by mesmerizing moments of watching the snow fall. During the first week of October, the snow began to accumulate, piling into a wall of ice. I had minimal warm clothing, just one pull-over and a light jacket that an aunt from the west coast generously mailed me. The closest Walmart was over forty miles away.

Winter in northern Michigan was quite the contrast to the tropical latitude I was used to. I had no idea about the forty feet of snow and minus forty degrees temperatures; the locals lovingly referred to their part of the world as "the freezer" of the United States. My tropically-thin blood was in shock, to say the least.

One particular Friday evening, I had used all the clothes out of my little suitcase and was down to what I was wearing. By a forced decision, I inquired about a place to launder my clothes. I was too freaked out to ask my housemates. I couldn't find the landlord, Ms. Selby, as she was on vacation in China. And I would not dare ask Mr. Eves. My "inn" mates told me about the little laundromat across the way, but I was suspicious of them. Did they do drugs? I finally broke down and asked the neighbors next door, who were the kindest people I had ever met.

I decided to drag my laundry in two big trash bags across town. The snow and wind picked up; my nose and hands were frozen to the point of intense, gnawing pain. So I walked into the grocery store with my laundry to find my cashier friend, Ms. Alessandra. She was a sweet girl who always had a smile glued to her face.

There weren't many people there, but the two who were shopping did care to stare at me and my two bags of laundry. I asked Alessandra for directions to the laundromat, as my directionally-challenged brain was frozen.

I got some change from her cashier stand and headed over to where she pointed. I walked the directions to finally find the laundromat tucked away on the southwest corner of the only gas station in town. I was greeted by an older woman with darker hair. She had olive skin that was slightly wrinkled. She appeared to be at least in her seventies, if not in her eighties.

"Hi, there! How can I help you?" the friendly, older woman said. "My name is Anna. I am from Italy. I immigrated to the U.S. at the age of sixteen. I have a feeling you are not from around here and are possibly about that age?!" Anna was right about the first part but just close to a decade off on my age.

Phew! What a sigh of relief to hear Anna relate to me. I was a speck of brown dust in the little white town. Anna was incredibly nice. While my month-long pile of laundry was washing and drying, I learned a lot about this amazing woman's life. She instantly took me in like a mother and a grandmother. I thought to myself, *What an angel!* She was God-sent—I had no other explanation.

Anna talked about her life as an immigrant, about how she learned English and about losing her husband, who had been in the military. She moved a lot as a child and as a grown adult. I could relate to Anna. She had a granddaughter that she dearly loved who was living with her and moving away to college soon. I almost took her place that evening. We shared our life stories like two long-lost friends. As we talked, Anna realized *where* I was staying.

Her kind and cheerful disposition changed quickly, deep-lined frowns appearing on her forehead, a look of concern coming from her emerald green eyes. She had questions streaked across her face. I could see the wheels turning in her head very fast because I shared her deep thoughts. Even before Anna put words to her thoughts, I knew she was concerned for me. "We need to get you out of there as quickly as possible!" Anna declared.

I thought, *What!?!*

Anna continued, "I am driving you over to see Mr. Jack Landings."

"Who is Mr. Jack Landings?" I asked.

She said, "He is my friend. I know he has a house he rents out, and I believe the upstairs is currently empty."

Was I supposed to worry about where I was living, or should I be relieved that this angel of a woman was going to find me a safe place to live soon? As we drove forty miles to see Mr. Landings, Anna filled me in with more of her life but also interjected and told me about how unsafe it was where I was staying. Fear gripped me instantly. Anna still refused to disclose details, but the thought of Mr. Eve's peering eyeballs and the others who lived there with their long, dreary eyes, smoke-filled apartments, and unkempt looks was enough for me to know she was right. It simply gave me the creeps.

I remembered a time at the "inn" when I just needed to send an email to my parents in Africa to let them know I was safely in the U.S. They were happy that I could now take care of everyone else financially, relieving them and my siblings of their miseries. My siblings were asking for money for a computer and a motor-bike, while I was fearfully knocking on my neighbors' door for internet access in order to send and receive an email.

I was in and out of their room as quick as I could be, my mind racing and my feet ready to make a mad dash for the exit. I profusely thanked them—they were beautiful human be-ings. But their room was smelly, littered with empty beer cans, half-eaten cans of soup, and sausages on the floor. Clothes were everywhere. I was suffocating from the stench of the room as I briskly left.

Anna's concerns came alive one more time in my head as I remembered back to that moment.

We finally arrived at Mr. Landings' place. He offered a new upstairs apartment of a three-bedroom house. I was thankful I could move into the apartment on the upper floor. Mr. Landings, Anna, and I drove to the apartment. To my viewing pleasure, a pale-yellow house with siding sat off the curb, crooked, looking like the Leaning Tower of Pisa. But it didn't matter at that point. Compared to what I would be leaving behind, this was a won-derful upgrade. Anna knew best, and I was grateful for this new possibility of moving into a safe space.

I did not have a phone. I asked Anna how I could purchase one. I had no bank account nor had I received my first paycheck from work. Anna told me she knew of a guy who could help. So she drove me to meet this man who sold me a used, large phone that looked more like a walkie talkie with an antenna than a cell phone. I was relieved, as I could call locally anywhere in the U.S. and Canada, and I could use a phone card and connect with the world again. My parents hadn't heard from me for a couple of months. I don't know how mother survived without providing me with all her *guidance* and *advice*. When I finally called her on my new phone, it hardly took her a day to catch up with parenting me by phone. Again!

Winter was approaching, and it was catching up with my sense of isolation and loneliness. Abandonment crept into my soul with a strong grip. Once my parents settled their anxiety, mine began to rise. The winter was setting in quickly, just like Anna had warned me. She nudged me to move as quickly as I could. Winters were blistering, harsh, and icy. And yet, minus forty-degree temperatures were nothing close to what my body had experienced in the past.

Although my past attachment wounds were influencing my life in the present, God's hand was on display through the many women, including sisters, mothers, and friends he was bringing into my life, while the river of my life meandered through the hills of Michigan.

The church on the hill became a sanctuary for me, especially on Wednesday and Saturday nights and Sunday mornings. If I did not show up to church, the girls would knock on my door every time to check in on me. I built deep friendships—Kelly, Leslie, Lori, and a few others became my tight-knit sisterhood.

I was part of the church family gatherings and picnics. Pastor Cook and his family treated me more like their own family. This was an unusual experience, and I felt undeserving of so much care, attention, and concern.

However, Anna's words rang in my ears, "Try to move from this small town. It's depressing when the dead of winter sets in. Move to where you have family." I took Anna at her word and contacted an employer in the big city of Chicago—at least I had family and a friend from my undergraduate program who lived in the Windy City. They could provide me with some support. My uncle who lived in Chicago drove to the small town in Michigan and picked me up, along with my few belongings, which consisted of a suitcase and a few boxes of books.

As I bid farewell to the little town and watched the trees in their brightest colors of fall on our drive to Chicago, I had only gratitude in my heart. I had made lifelong friendships with sisters, mothers, and daughters. I witnessed God's heart pursue me through these relationships. My uncle and his family were incredibly gracious; I stayed with them for a few weeks. My thoughtful cousins ensured I knew how to get around independently, and they oriented me to life in the big city. They were big brothers to me. My uncle and aunt took me around as I tried to find an apartment to move into after I got my first paycheck from my new job. Their family was like a breath of fresh air.

My job involved driving around in the treacherous Chicago winter, about 150-200 miles a day, in snowstorms and blizzards. With my directionally-challenged brain, I got lost numerous times. A time or two I ended up on the border of Indiana and in the unsafe parts of the city. My anxiety levels and loneliness skyrocketed. The first six months was a huge adjustment as I attempted to find my way around and do life in the big city. It certainly took a lot of energy from me. After a few months of my professional clinical fellowship year, I changed jobs. I did not know how to negotiate a salary and received my paychecks gratefully. I later learned that I was extremely under-compensated.

It was about this time that I was bombarded with marriage proposals again. The same story on repeat; I was too old, according to Mom. She reminded me that I would have loose teeth and dentures soon. I had to settle down quickly before I became a loser and life would treat me very harshly.

After a few weeks of this, I was told that I was abandoning my parents since I hadn't called them. To Mom, I was living my life on a bed of roses and had forgotten about all the sacrifices they made for me. I was made to listen to how I wasn't fulfilling the role of a good and responsible daughter. My labels of *abandoner and abuser of parents* fluctuated, so I laid down the rule—one more time—that they were not going to find me a match, that I would definitely say No!

⟡

Looking back, I know that God was with me. He did not abandon me. Instead, he loved me with reckless abandon. As I traveled around in my little Saturn, I experienced his hand of love, his protection, and his presence as I cried many tears and prayed many prayers. My day began at four in the morning and often ended close to midnight. There were many occasions I felt that God had shown up tangibly through a person or in protection over my life from intruders, gangs, snow, ice storms, and blizzards. Although my brain was in a state of hyper-alertness, I arrived home safely every night. That gave me assurance that God heard my relentless prayers every time! This grounded my belief that he was real.

∽

Reflection Questions

Do you remember a time when, in the midst of all the dysfunctional relationships, you saw or met someone who cared about you and modeled family and relationships differently than you had previously experienced?

Have you ever considered looking back in the rearview mirror of your life and recalling those Canaan moments—streams in the desert—and writing them down?

Can you think of something to practice gratitude for even in the midst of circumstances that feel overwhelming? It will rewire your brain, and your brain will eventually help you start searching out positive experiences in your environment and relationships. Brain science attests to this. David in the Psalms practiced this.

~⑤

Words of encouragement

David lamented about his heart's condition in most of his psalms; however, he ends by identifying a character of God to be thankful for, and he verbalized it out loud, sometimes even "cried" it out.

Our brains are much more neuro-plastic than we ever dreamed of. Novelty and creativity are possible with neuro-genesis (growth of new brain cells) and these cells link-up to form synaptic connections and neural networks for both our positive and negative thoughts. There is hard scientific evidence indicating that one hour of focusing on a thought can double the synaptic connections of cells to build up neural muscle.

Billions of neurons are either busy tearing apart or rewiring based on what we pay attention to in our environmental and relational fields. When we stop paying attention to that critical voice in our head, we don't use those connections and they wither away. We also stop making them.

When we stop telling ourselves, "I am not good enough," and replace that lie with a truth statement like, "I am good enough and worthy of connection, care, nurturing, and healthy relationships," the brain stops sending messages to our senses to look for evidence of confirmation. We template match—looking at our experiences, we try to match the statement with our past experiences. When the critical voice in our head says, "You don't belong," then we try to not include ourselves in a group because it is safer. We don't have to be vulnerable, rejected, or disappointed. But, on the other hand, if we face our lie statements with intention, choice, and acknowledgment, that can lead us to face our core issues and deal with them.

୨

Final Note

In the process of my life's journey, there was a lot of separation from family by circumstances, not necessarily by choice but from their blindness to the brokenness of it all. One thing after another resulted in deepening my mother-wounds. But I was on the run, I was in search of home (wholeness) for which I needed to leave home. I had to "undo" my old belief templates and replace them with new truths. David, in the Psalms, cries out to God while experiencing deep emotions of anger, fear, sadness, and shame. Every feeling word you can think of, he experienced and expressed it. But he also experienced joy, praise, and jubilation.

This book of Psalms in the Bible is ancient Israel's book of emotions and prayers and also became my book of emotional prayer and praise. I expressed my feelings and emotions *raw, but I had to deliberately shift my perspective to praise. Yes, I had to neurobiologically shift my perspective! But it takes intentionality and practice to create new, healthy relationships. I had to apply this "unconditional" perspective to my emotions and new relationships. And I did it.*

I hope and pray that you can, too!

Chapter 12

◦⽊

IS MY HEART AT
HOME YET?

*"Home is a place not only of strong affections
but of entire unreserve; it is life's undress
rehearsal, its backroom, its dressing room."*

—Harriet Beecher Stowe

S afety is learned primarily through the mother-child relationship. The child is completely dependent on the mother to
help them deal with the childhood emotions of anxiety, rage,
loneliness, fear, and insecurities that are potentially overwhelming. A mother holding her child's emotional experience is a critical factor in the child's development. When there is a mal-attach-
ment between parent and child, the child's subsequent grownup
ability to regulate his or her own adult emotional life is affected,
and intimate relationships are impacted. As Pamela J. Conrad
puts it.

"For most, home is the steady center of life. It is the comfort zone where we return for refueling, emotional support, and privacy. Home is the place to disengage from structure and authority. It is a focal point to bring balance into your life."

—Pamela J. Conrad,
Balancing Home & Career

I was still wandering through life, wondering if there was a way back home, a place to arrive, a state to achieve. In this chapter, I will show you how I found myself in cyclical patterns that brought me back full circle right to where I had begun, in the deep agony of soul wounding, including spiritual abuse. I was still searching for freedom from this broken mother-child relationship

❦

"Your sickness and your children's sickness are consequences of how you are treating your parents." "You deserve it." "God is teaching you a good lesson!" "You are not in submission… to me." "God's word says you need to honor your parents." "I hope your children won't treat you the way you are treating me." These were frequent comments I heard from my mom during my early years of child-rearing. She constantly pointed out that I had a problem with "dishonoring" parents. This sentiment was conveyed by many extended family members through the grapevine or directly to me. And, at times, I even heard this from my younger siblings. Many folks were singing the same old song.

According to my mother, I was a drama queen with an emotional or anger problem. I reacted too much or I was being silly. I was determined to establish boundaries for self-protection as I knew it then. Little did I realize that I was letting my family "get to me" as I reacted or walled myself off, behaving the way they wanted me to.

I began battling hard to identify who I was and how I got to this level of dysfunction in my relationship with my mother. I knew that I had to create a separate identity from her and from the codependent relationship that we had. I would swing like a pendulum from establishing boundaries to walling her completely off so that I could have my own space to breathe. Then I would feel guilty and fall prey to the guilt-trip trap where I would allow Mom to emotionally blackmail, manipulate or gaslight me. I would then feel ashamed of myself, feel compassion for my mom, and resume talking with her.

My poor mom must have spent a lot of energy trying to keep this crazy dynamic going... I couldn't live without this relationship. I was living in a vortex with my mother, repeating the same patterns of behavior in relating to her as a grown adult even while raising my own children. However dysfunctional this relationship was, *my need to connect* with my own mother took me back to the one whose DNA I shared. I was like the woman who went back to her abusive husband.

I questioned myself and my identity as an adult, and I realized that I had many labels I adopted along the way. The title "abandoner of family" won every time I tried to separate or voice the dysfunction of Mom's control or manipulation over me. Over and over again I fell back into the trap of being a "rescuer." I understood my roles as a surrogate mom who rescued my siblings and surrogate spouse to my dad, which filled his emotional needs because mother couldn't or didn't know how to. If I didn't fulfill these roles then I was called an abuser! If I made any excuses, I was "ungrateful" for everything they had done for me to get me to this point in my life, and I was selfish and certainly the black sheep of the family. I was perfectly enacting the *drama triangle* as I swayed between the victim, rescuer, and prosecutor.[15]

A couple of years ago, I had to let Mom know that we wouldn't be making a trip to India just yet. We had made four trips in four years, two of which I made to see my dad at the hospital, as he required two brain tumor removals eighteen months apart. Prior to that, we had traveled as a family to India for my grandfather's ninetieth birthday, and a few years later, over a one-year period, we traveled to visit family and then to attend my brother's wedding in India.

This time, however, I had just gone through surgery to address fast-growing fibroids, which made my uterus the size of a five-month pregnant woman. My child had suffered from pneumonia off and on for almost nine months leading up to my surgery. And these life events simply took priority over planning a summer trip to India.

During many conversations with my mom, I felt obligated to give an explanation as to why I couldn't come to see my parents right away. Financially, we were drained by myriad medical expenses and four previous trips halfway around the globe (those tickets aren't cheap).

To all of this, Mother said the following: "Well, you know your disabled dad wants to see you." "Stop mistreating him and making him suffer emotionally." "Stop abusing Daddy."

She even manipulated me, stating that my disabled father's condition was declining so fast that they were considering putting him on hospice. I found myself providing explanations to convince Mom as to why I couldn't come despite me feverishly wanting to. I knew Dad was declining post brain tumor removal and radiation treatments. To make matters worse, his neurological disease MSA-P (Multiple system atrophy, Parkinsonian type-a neurological degenerative disorder) was progressing. The MSA-P diagnosis was complicating his post-tumor recovery; he was quickly losing his abilities with posture, balance, movement, speech, and swallowing.

The barrage continued. "You are not doing your duty as a daughter; you call yourself spiritual?" At some point, Mom even told me I didn't have enough Jesus in me to behave like a Christian. I just couldn't bear the torture of hearing how much I had *abandoned* them.

One of the reasons that I believe God led me to become a speech pathologist and swallowing therapist was for my father. I advocated for his protection and dignity. All my professional skills came in handy at the hospital and with his recovery at home afterward. However, Mother was angry with me when I couldn't video call three to four times a week to provide him with speech therapy, even though I was in touch with the therapist who provided services. I gave my mom and the therapist practical tips. However, I could not be my dad's therapist. This was a familiar pattern. I was blamed for not emotionally caretaking in this situation or coming home to India again during this time of tribulation.

Mom told me that I "could have my surgery and then come over and 'heal' with them!" She wanted me to sacrifice my health and my family's health to take care of her situation. What a double bind! I concluded that I was never good enough and could never perform well enough to be the daughter that Mom wanted me to be, the *good-enough* girl who went along with the plan. I could never satisfy her. Anything I did or said would never be enough!

∽

Mom was always concerned with how much time I spent caring for my kids, claiming that it was too much and the extra attention was unnecessary. Mother constantly advised me that I needed to get a Ph.D. and find a teaching job rather than waste my life. I had sacrificed a full-time career to be available and present for my chronically-ill children for over a decade. I worked part-time gigs on the weekends and multiple on-call jobs during the week when my children were in school and whenever circumstances permitted me to make it work.

Who was I? A ragdoll fulfilling ten different roles? *Every aspect of my life including my parenting was inadequate or insufficient. I felt like I couldn't live my own life without feeling guilty for living and parenting.* If I traveled on vacation or did something fun, I felt like I was wasting money on myself—it was full-blown insanity.

Where were these thoughts coming from? I had a lack of emotional freedom to live my life separated from my mom... I heard my aunts and other mother figures say how selfish I was, despite all the sacrifices my parents made on my behalf. These sentiments were thrown in my face even now as an adult. My inner critical judging voice harped at me saying, "How dare you live your life?" and "Who do you think you are?" My own lies

184

and the belief systems that I had established unconsciously— my implicit memories (memories we have stored unconsciously that causes us to feel the emotions, but have no memory of the event)—and my limbic system were driving my behavior patterns and my choices.

I had a poor self-image, a lack of self-worth and little compassion for myself. Instead, I hated myself and my own critical voice, which had become my identity. It was beginning to harness and control me. I had been emotionally, physically, and spiritually keeping score of all the lies that were magnified.

I had to start somewhere to answer the question of who I was. I realized that I wasn't caring for my soul by self-critiquing and inflicting these burdens on myself in order to save the ancestral family. I was so frustrated by *trying* to keep it all together for everyone, everywhere. This was the ultimate crazy-making! Based on the family system, cultural system, religious and educational systems that I was influenced and controlled by, I had developed a belief system of lies that established themselves as my inner truths. Although I was lonely, I realized I was strong, dependable, reliable, responsible, competent, and self-sufficient. I recognized these qualities in my character even though I was the object of harsh criticism. Finally, I made an unwavering decision to find *real* truth.

I went on a quest to discover who I was and whom I was meant to be. Did I have an authentic self—a real me? Who was that person? What was I created for? The stories of my life hadn't lined up for four decades to provide me with answers. I was sick and tired of those inner voices, so I decided to challenge them! I had to find another way out.

Dr. Stephen Porges, in his Polyvagal Theory, talks about circuits in our autonomous nervous system that are constantly looking for cues that trigger "neuroception" (our nervous system's evaluation of risk to protect us from threat of safety, danger, and life threat.)[16] Even at a primitive brain level function, the removal of threat does not suffice. We require *safety* for social engagements. We cannot connect and co-regulate with another human being if there is no safety in the relationship. And according to Dr. Porges, this is how we are wired neurologically, beginning at the very primitive levels of our brain.

A divine God wired in us an innate biological template that desires a safe and secure connection with another. When a young child experiences the emotions of intense fear, helplessness or horror, and doesn't have language or thoughts to process them, this leads to the creation of traumatic events that lead to emotions that get burned into the child's nervous system. Very young children are operating at an instinctual level with their need for feelings to be understood or contained by an adult until they can do it themselves. Young children, as I've mentioned in earlier chapters, are completely dependent on parents or caretakers to intuitively sense their vulnerabilities, notice their feelings, and put them into perspective with language and emotional containment.

It is no surprise that when a traumatic environment is present, primitive agonies of childhood are survived and carried into adulthood. Most parents work hard to protect their children from the inherent emotional instabilities of life; however, if our traumatized states found no welcoming, relational home or were not given voice, then they got stuffed inside or pushed to the side.

We resort to strategies of shutting down, avoiding the pain, or we make ourselves more rigid on the inside. We tense up, soldier ourselves, or devote our desperate and helpless selves to work or family; we may even end up drowning ourselves in addictions to numb the pain.

As adults, these offending and threatening feelings are literally buried, but the sad fact is they are still there and are triggered by events. They grab us when we are not looking. Symptoms may look like an undercurrent of our emotions on nerve fibers, firing faster than our thoughts, weaving through every aspect of our lives. In an effort to protect ourselves from the effects, we shut ourselves off to the potential connections we are wired for. Traumatic events impact us even if we do not want them to. We can't think our way out of a traumatic event or skirt around it. The rational part of us cannot avoid the impacts. It comes like a thief in the night!

Even if we don't experience natural disasters or man-made catastrophes, we are inevitably going to face or be confronted with death, serious injury, illness, or threats to our own loved one's integrity in this fallen world. Even if we make it through traumatic events in our childhood or adolescence in one piece, the glass is already broken.

> When I finally looked at the broken shards of my childhood, every minute facing it became sacred; the broken pieces in the fallenness of my life became unavoidable.

Trauma happens all around us; it is a fact of everyday life. Offenses against us, including our self-inflicted offenses, will eventually touch us or someone else if it hasn't already. Early traumas restrict our abilities to process later traumatic events. Early emotional rapport or lack thereof lives into adulthood.

No parent is perfect. It is in the repair—in an environment of love—that mends the failure with "good enough parenting." When this isn't the case, it leads to mother (or father) void-ness and attachment issues.

In my case, I was the mad child, alone and looking for a long-lost mother. I could never find her. I was with her, yet it seemed like I could never find that *kind* mother I was searching for. It was as if she was hiding! There was a breakdown in that intrinsic, God-ordained, dynamic parent-child engagement that was meant to support and facilitate my normal social, emotional, and spiritual development. There was estrangement and aloneness, which I was still experiencing in adulthood. I was grieving someone who was still alive. I was grieving as an adult. My childhood wounds swelled up like the womb of a pregnant woman. I was looking for a place to arrive, a state to achieve, I was looking to find "home" again. I was searching for relief from developmental and relational traumas created by the wounds of the trauma of "mother lies." Lies that I heard and lived with that added to this moment of my identity crisis. I saw myself through the lens of others who didn't see value or worth in me.

With the help of my therapist, I realized that my insecure attachments had led to terrible problems within and all around me. I had difficulty in relationships.

As you have read my story, you must have already figured out my disordered and dysfunctional childhood attachment and insecurity. I did not have enough secure attachment or bonding in my relational experiences as a young child. I did not have the cognition or the language to understand or explain it then.

I had problems creating trustworthy bonding for future relationships; in friendships, work relationships, with my spouse, and even my children. I didn't have consistent attachment figures in my life who spoke the language of secure attachment and the normal bonding process besides Grandma Sara and a few other loving relationships. They were streams in the desert, yet too short-lived to quench my thirst in the dry, cracked, parched land of my mother-void and attachment needs. I simply didn't have reliable tools to manage significant relationships cognitively or emotionally at home, work, or play.

After years of therapy, a journey through self-discovery, journaling, praying, and understanding my own neurobiology of trauma and dysfunction, I grasped how my childhood traumas had impacted my adult life. I came to the scientific conclusion that I was carrying life's hurts and soul wounding in the very fabric of who I was.

I have learned from my therapists and through my life experiences that I could re-learn and master healthy, secure attachment. It has been a process, and it will continue to be a lifelong process. It will never be perfect. There is nothing that will ever be perfect until we are in heaven, but in the meantime, we can use our grace-made, God-given opportunities to heal.

My own search for answers from my personal childhood trauma, fortunately, led me to many therapeutic interventions and recovery groups for relational brokenness where I began a journey of healing. I tried to utilize my adult cognition and intelligence to understand my experiences — how this had formed and shaped me as a person. I diligently researched the bodywork of trauma resolution and attended therapy for several years.

I identified and understood that connecting relationally to myself and others was a complex idea. The traumas I had experienced cut me off from other people in my life, my creativity, my purpose, and ultimately from God my creator.

I now needed to focus on restoring connection after feeling so isolated through developmental trauma. I was determined to find a therapist who could show me how to heal my disruptions. This trauma work was critical to my relational health. It was essential for me to understand how to *overcome* my developmental emotional trauma because we don't just get over deep, soul attachment wounding by just working on our thoughts.

You need to go to someone who knows how to help you understand attachment styles and to teach you how to move toward secure attachment. Even better is finding someone who is reflective of and who has worked through their own attachment history. Someone who has walked the journey and not just talked about the journey.

A word of caution: a well-intentioned but uninformed therapist can actually negatively impact your healing journey. You'll need to research and even ask if they have experience in working with clients with attachment issues or attachment-informed therapies for adults.

Why? Because by learning and mastering healthy and secure attachments, it will help us with our relationships to connect more effectively and enable us to have a deep, meaningful relationship with others.

I have been deeply influenced and helped by the work of researchers Diane Poole Heller,[17] Dan Siegel,[18] and Allan Schore[19] in the fields of science and neurobiology of attachment. They have convinced me that although our early wounding occurred developmentally, we can heal from it. Allan Schore says, "Ninety percent of what's going in our adult relationships stem from our attachment history." Hopefully, we can find a therapist who practices attachment therapy, helping us move toward secure attachment in our emotions, language, and behavior. According to John Bowlby, secure attachment is in our biological design.

My mother used to tell me as a child that they as parents worked very hard to provide a roof over my head, put food on the table, and invest in a great education, and that I should be very "grateful." I am grateful for all their financial sacrifices and the opportunities I've had in life because of their sacrifices. Secure attachment is a lot more than having a roof over our heads, being taken to the doctor when we were sick or providing us with three meals a day. What really helps us heal our attachment deficits is compassionate, loving contact with others who can love us non-judgmentally, without shame and blame.

The following are the four different attachment styles:

Secure: This is the experience of trust, relaxation in relationships, easy flow of connection and aloneness when we are children. It includes parental protection, playfulness, predictable safety, and trust, which is much needed for our development. We are confident enough to explore the world around us. We are seen and heard and our emotions matter to the world around us. We can reasonably and confidently ask for our needs to be met, and we have the capacity to meet others' needs. Very few of us had this kind of secure attachment when we were children. That is why we then developed other adaptive attachment styles.

Avoidant: As a child, if our experience was that no one was really present as a parent or caregiver, we learn this second attachment style of avoidance. We retreat back into ourselves in isolation, as we have nothing really to attach to due to the neglect of being left alone or actively rejected too much as a child. We learn to not need anything from anyone.

Ambivalent: This third style emerges from the "She loves me, she loves me not" internal dilemma. With this style, there is a dynamic of an on-again, off-again kind of inconsistent love that creates crushing anxiety. We long for deep love from others, but at the very same time, we have a disabling fear of losing it. I wasn't sure if good mommy or bad mommy would show up! We develop this internal tug of war, due to our experiences of inconsistent love from our early attachment figures.

Disorganized: Yep, it's exactly what the word means: a disorganized mess of confusing and disorienting style of adaptation. We fall into this approach if we perceive our parent as scared or scary, but the instinctual drive for bonding and survival drives us toward closeness with them. We require help, but in seeking the help, we often end up defending ourselves—a perfect setup for the freeze response. The disorganized-attached person may be avoidant for a moment, but the need for secure attachment pulls them to seek it, yet they may then become ambivalent the next moment.

Personally, I fell into this disorganized category. I oscillated between avoidant and ambivalent. These patterns are pre-verbally and pre-cognitively learned. I wasn't conscious about this until I did the sacred and transformational work of learning secure attachment in therapy and recovery groups. Through therapy, I renewed the template of my relational blueprint that I unconsciously learned as a child. I learned the language of secure attachment that is primarily the "language of love." I addressed traumatic events in my implicit memory (unconscious memory). I learned the "gaps" in my attachment history and changed the code in the vault of my inherent blueprint of disorganized attachment. I accessed the source of my wounding and let myself know I wasn't crazy.

What was especially true of my injury was the lack of development due to the deficits in my care early on. As you have read throughout my story, even after I left home, I was still responding to events that occurred twenty, thirty, and forty years prior. And I know many people out there are still responding to events from years ago as I did.

The things we hear from society and the lessons we learned from our previous experiences can hold us back in the present. For example, my experience of stage fright—that fifth-grade event where I swallowed my words during my vocal performance contributed to my belief system. It was a lie that grew tentacles in my brain; reception of fear and conditioned anxiety that I was not good at public speaking and that I would never speak in public again. These moments in time feel like they define who we are, those experiences we hold on to become so ingrained in us that we can't let them go. They become our limiting beliefs. Part of me knew my core issues and wanted to change. I wanted to improve core relationships.

Our amygdala (the part of the brain that focuses solely on our survival) stores this energy in the form of ancient mechanisms God created at the neural level—the body determines we are not safe, and we hit the fight, flight, or freeze state to survive. The amygdala essentially determines what we should fight for, what we should flee from and what is so terrifying that we should freeze rendering us incapable of responding. We are suddenly taken over by our limbic brain and our creativity is arrested. Our cortex, specifically our frontal brain, goes offline. We begin to operate under this conditioned exacerbation of fear and danger. And we believe something is wrong. It is biologically impossible to feel critical of ourselves and at the same time make an open-hearted connection with another human being.

There are many limbic system therapies out there. You have to research and choose one or any combination of these therapies to break the power of the limbic system, your nervous system, and intrinsic body memories.

One specific therapy I went through was *attachment-focused* EMDR (Eye Movement Desensitization and Reprocessing). This is a well- researched, specialized trauma therapy performed by a mental health professional who has very specific training. This trauma therapy uses alternating movements. I can attest to the fact that this technique works very well for post-traumatic stress. It really helped me deal with my childhood traumas and wounding that were deeply seated in my limbic system. The therapist had my eyes move far left, far right, or sometimes other bilateral stimulation like tapping right-left, right-left on my knees or even have me listening to sounds left-right. EMDR activated rapid neurobiological processing of disturbing memories that had been stuck in my mind and body that begin to move out. In psychological terms, my therapist called this "memory reconsolidation."

She explained, "You have thoughts and feelings and body sensations that you reprocess as memory that are filed away. When you bring up these memories after EMDR therapy, you can remember events without causing you to emotionally fall apart."

I am a Christian and I believe in the redeeming power of an Almighty God. I found a therapist who shared my faith and values, and we invited the Holy Spirit to come and meet me in my emotions. Through this work, I was set free in my emotions, although I did not forget the traumatic events. I have been able to write and speak about these events without my emotions taking over, which is real healing. I was able to fully embrace God and the power of His word. The fog cleared, the clouds parted, and I began to see and hear God again.

I adopted practical tools and biblical resources that helped me heal, therefore preventing me from passing down these traumas to my children. I was able to focus on and practice healthy parenting, following God's blueprint for family—secure attachment. I am in no way claiming perfect parenting; however, I was able to break the cycle of the dysfunction and abuse I had experienced. Why am I emphasizing early attachments, science, and neurobiology? There is *hope* for us. We are not too far gone for transformation, redemption, and wholeness. I personally believe that is the ultimate divine plan for us as individuals, families, communities, and even as nations! We can't change or work on anything we are not aware of.

What was once disrupted in early relationships needs to be healed through loving, trustworthy relationships.

Years later, I am still working on becoming free by working on the unintegrated, wounded parts of me created by the difficult experiences of my childhood stored in the limbic parts of my brain. All too often, my limbic system where those memories were stored was running my life, running the show behind the scenes. Thankfully, I learned that I can relax and also restore connection in trustworthy relationships—my attachment-focused therapist, other mom figures, women's recovery groups, and friends became my loving circle for practicing healthy relating.

I did develop intimate friendships once I learned to be secure, real, and authentic. I saw my safe mothers, sisters, and brothers model it for me. I am learning to trust incrementally, slowly building a foundation for healthy relating and relationships. The circle of friendships I have developed currently is fun, loving, and humorous. I had to tell myself that I wasn't too broken to be restored. I challenged the lies and broken belief systems. Something was finally changing in me from the inside out. I have learned that I can bring my true, authentic self into the world and not feel ashamed or guilty of who I am. That is God's idea for healing and recovery from any type of traumatic event in our life.

Reflection Questions

Have you had limiting beliefs about yourself, voices that told you that you were not good enough, smart enough, or capable enough, and have you carried those lies with you into adulthood?

Have you had self-sabotaging tapes, voices that play over and over again to the point that the messages owned you?

Have you thought that these voices defined or overtook everything you ever wanted to do and you felt like a deflated balloon? Did this get to the point of arresting your thought process and your dreams for the future?

❧

Words of encouragement

For me, even the thought of being published, being seen out there in the world, felt like I was betraying my family, my mother, and my mothering figures. Most of all, it felt like I was betraying myself. This thought was terrifying. We don't want to face our root fears — the root of our self-sabotage. We need to deconstruct that self-sabotaging, illogical decision.

God had different plans for me, although he moved me around. He permitted a nomadic existence and my suffering through my early attachment wounding. I just needed to trust this recovery journey.

Let us visit scripture for a moment. The Bible has many references about "connection": to not give up meeting regularly (Hebrews 10:25), to carry each other's burdens (Galatians 6:2). God is a relational being; He deeply cared for **fellowship** *and* **connection**, *so he created Adam — the first man. God walked and talked with Adam in the garden. He knew Adam was alone and he needed a real human (flesh and blood) connection. God knew he was enough, but he also knew his created being Adam required a real-life person to heal his loneliness.*

God cares about your attachments. That is why he put us in a family, a community, and a tribe to walk together and heal. Sometimes that means seeing a therapist, partner-

ing with a safe person who will stick with you with their presence, who will nurture you while holding and containing your wounds. As you transform those broken and disintegrated parts of yourself, you develop more security and resiliency in relationships. With a sense of deep presence from safe people, we are nourished by positive bonding, as God intended.

~☺~

Final Note

Embrace where you are, even if you can't feel, hear, or see any light at the end of your deep, dark tunnel. We can learn to embrace and honor our trauma. I learned to not avoid it anymore, deny it, or minimize it, or even think I was making it up—that it was a dream, that this couldn't have really happened to me.

I had resorted to all of the above and by so doing, lost myself. I put everybody on the priority list—their feelings and emotions. I was doing what they wanted me to do and felt what they wanted me to feel. I thought, "How can you take care of yourself or your family? Your sick children or your own illness—your immune system dysfunction—before you take care of others?" I had always believed that I was selfish to take care of myself and my family, but not anymore. I gave myself permission to feel my emotions.

When you minimize your story, you minimize your life. Don't live under the weight of someone else's perspective. God gave us language and emotions to express ourselves. I encourage you, too—to give yourself permission to complete any unfinished business that you may have in your attachment history so you can enjoy life-giving, fulfilling relationships that are meaningful now and moving forward.

Chapter 13

⟳

My Spiritual Awakening —Image Bearer?

"So God created mankind in his own image; in his own image God created them; He created them male and female."

—Genesis 1:27 (ISV)

"A time for everything; for everything there is a season, and a time for every matter under heaven...a time to heal, a time to break down, and a time to build up..."

—Ecclesiastes 3:3 (ESV)

Going through therapy, understanding early traumatic events, and processing it in a safe environment with safe adults, including my therapist and groups, was necessary. I had detested myself as a woman, and the terribly wounded inner child in me was now in the healing process. However, I needed a spiritual answer to my experiences and the misery that I had experienced.

The feminine characters in my life had betrayed me. My mother, and other mothering figures, had failed me. I had been attacked by women—physically, emotionally, spiritually, and even sexually. Everything that constitutes womanhood was challenged by another significant woman in my life. Once I got to a place that calmed my dissociated and disconnected brain and I had my mind (cognitive frontal parts of my brain) free to think again, I was ready to question where God was in all of this. This chapter is an attempt to show you that although I saw myself as a "hot mess express," God had been carrying me the whole time.

Although my purpose was stolen, I had this awakening in my soul—my traumatic events and the process of trauma resolution was a fast track to my spiritual growth.

For several decades of my life, I was bearing an image of the one who brought me into this world: my mother. But I was bearing a wounded image. And I did not want to become an image bearer of wounds to my children, particularly my daughter.

I questioned if my mother was wounded. There is a saying in the therapeutic community that "hurt people hurt people," consciously or unconsciously. I knew I was unconsciously bearing an image of someone in my body, soul, emotions, and my spirit. The family image, mother image, and all the other "images" that had been given to me were not working. There had to be another image I could bear—one I was meant to bear. An image of *wholeness*.

I began to explore the key to my spiritual freedom by answering this crucial question: Whose image am I bearing? Yes, that included my fragile self-worth, self-esteem, and body image. Earthly images had ruined me, failed and betrayed me. I had to look to an image higher than myself or anyone I knew—a divine, supernatural, and unadulterated image that could give me value and worth. This was a journey to the reclamation of who I was really meant to be. If God created me in the sacred, divine place of the womb, then wasn't I an image bearer of the Creator?

I had learned that I was created by purpose, as I was on His mind before the foundations of the worlds, *on purpose by his idea, by specific design, for purpose.*

All these years, I had never considered God anything besides male—authoritative, punishing, fierce, majestic, kingly, and of course, in my early years, as Father. Whose image was I supposed to be bearing in womanhood and in motherhood?

I began exploring this concept of what it meant to be an image bearer after four decades of life. Let's go back to the creation story in Genesis 1:26-27.

"And then God said let us make mankind in our image." When God said, "in our image," he created them male and female. God created us man and woman and placed us side-by-side in equal purpose and calling. And one day I had an aha God-moment. It struck me—we bear the image of God. Yes, as both male and *female*!

I had to encounter and wrestle with the God of the Universe to believe that in my femaleness I am God's image bearer. When

God created man, he created them both in His image, male and female. Male is only half the equation. We are complete as his image bearer when the image of God is represented as a woman. I got it. God represents both male and female in the creation story.

In the creation story, God created Eve as a suitable helper. In Hebrew, the word is "Ezer" (one who is like God, created in his image). I also realized that I do bear the image of those I hang out with. The book of John says, "In the beginning was the word, the word was with God, the word is God." As I began to hang out with the God of the Universe through his "Word," I understood that I too am called "Ezer" by the One whose name is Ezer (helper). I began to understand God's heart *that helps* through the pages of scripture. He wanted to be my helper who walked alongside me. I understood him as a warrior—he fights for me. Jehovah Ezer became the Lord, my help.

All this while, I had seen myself as a wounded child, but now I embraced my new name and identity as Ezer—a fighter, a warrior woman on the journey of healing!

When I began to look at myself through God's eyes, I began to look like a healed warrior woman rather than a wounded child. God was in the business of being my helpmate, with wisdom revealing himself and bringing order to my inner chaos. He began to meet the needs of my mother-void. My mother failed to protect me and to give me worth, but God showed me through his Word that he created me in his image with *inherent worth* as an Ezer. Bearing God's image also means we have inherent and immeasurable worth.

Let us consider the concept of worth and value for a moment. In ancient times, coins were imprinted with images of kings, emperors, and rulers. All money had an image that gave it value. Even today, all currency has value, regardless of where you are in the world.

As we look through the landscape of the Bible, besides the barter system in the Old Testament, which was the main form of currency in the form of goat, sheep or cattle, precious metals were often used. Weights and measures are recorded in gold and silver, for example, the Shekel, which was a set standard of weight. Abraham is recorded to have made several transactions using the Shekel. The word Shekel appears eighty-four times in the Old Testament, in addition to other currencies in the barter system. In 2 Kings 5, Naaman attempts to pay Elisha by offering him 10 talents of silver and 6,000 shekels of gold.

As economics and governments progressed, it became necessary to carry out transactions in representative money with the seal of the government guaranteeing the value of the coin. Money in the form of coins had intrinsic value and carried additional value on the authority of the government. The Greeks were early pioneers of coinage, their system of coinage spread across the Mediterranean region and became the standard trade routes at the time. The Jews would have first come in contact with these coins while in Babylonian and Assyrian captivity. In essence, coins were stamped with value and had inherent worth, but they also told a story. The metal and inscriptions tell about the affluence of people. Coins also declared power and told of victories.

Between the Old Testament and the New Testament, the Jews were allowed to mint their own coinage, but it was limited. They could not mint gold or silver coinage that would conflict with political powers that controlled them. So when we look at the coins of the Bible, we see the perfection of details (story) and *inherent value* contained within it. Isn't the same true of current times? I cannot print money and give it any value.

I learned something from this revelation. I have value because I am impressed upon with the image of God, with no greater value imprinted upon me than the Creator of the Universe and the highest authority. I have inherent worth! As a woman, I realized I am a co-creator with God. We, women, are amazing in that we are co-creators with God. Let me tell you the obvious why: there is no human creation, man or woman, brought into this world unless it grew in the womb of a woman, birthed by a woman. If you are human, you were birthed by a woman! God sent His only begotten Son, who was fully God and fully man, through the womb of a woman. He shared her DNA!

Since we bear the image of God, we have unmatched dignity. We are priceless. We have inherent worth and dignity. We are invaluable and irreplaceable. We are one of a kind, even among seven billion people. We are worthy of honor and the highest affection of the only One. We are called to protect the dignity of others as image bearers. And that means it matters how we treat others and ourselves—the image bearers of God. Yes, it matters how we treat ourselves, too. I was very good at being unkind to myself, mistreating and dishonoring myself. It also matters how others treat us. We have a choice to let others treat us with value and inherent worth. If we don't, we are dishonoring God by marring him who created his people in *his image*.

Our number one battlefield is in our minds. Did you know that we think about 50,000 to 70,000 thoughts a day? There is power in thought! Philippians 4:8 (NIV) says, "Finally, brothers and sisters, whatever is true, whatever is noble, whatever is right, whatever is pure, whatever is lovely, whatever is admirable—if anything is excellent or praiseworthy—think about such things."

I needed to defy my thoughts with truth. I didn't need to be locked down with my thoughts of being a wounded child. I am an Ezer! Yes, an image bearer of God, with inherent value and worth and dignity stamped on me by him.

I began to speak this out loud to my soul until it *felt* true. I began to say it to others.

As I began to transition from wounded image bearer to a restored Ezer, I realized the truth that God sees me in wounded-ness as an Ezer. I also began to see all the other Ezers in the Bible.

In Genesis, God *calls* Eve a wounded Ezer out of hiding. In Hagar, He *sees* an abandoned Ezer. In Hannah, he *heard* a grief-stricken, hope-ridden Ezer. In the New Testament, he saw, heard, and touched wounded Ezers with healing and wholeness. Christ always honored the women in his stories, their voices, and their hearts. They were never forgotten. They *always* belonged. Christ didn't degrade women; He honored women in their pain because he saw in them a restored Ezer. When he talked to them, he called them by name: *daughter*.

He revealed himself to them with promises of a God who never leaves their side; a God who hears their groans; and a God who remembers his promises: that she is *seen* and *known*, she *belongs*, and she is *beloved*. God's answer to the first problem of loneliness was a woman. He also made sure every woman knows she is never less than. Women do hard and holy things, including giving birth to the sons and daughters of man. God gave *wisdom* and *courage* to Deborah, and fierce courage and *strength* to Esther to risk it.

~⊙~

Reflection Questions

Have you ever considered you have inherent worth and dignity just as you are?

Have you ever thought, "If only I were smarter, or prettier, or thinner, or had a different skin color, or (fill in the blank)"?

Have you tried to change something about you, for example, attempting to do the hard, disciplined work of trying to lose weight or trying to heal your own pain and then you were beat up over it by yourself or others because you didn't produce those results?

*Let me tell you, I did, too, until my crazy became safe and predictable. I had walked those streets of "Crazy Town." I knew every inch of that town, the name of every street in my sleep. I ran laps around Crazy Town, particularly up and down the street named Shame. Do you know what I mean? That very familiar walk of shame? That very strong sense of making shame your identity? Yes, that stronghold that tells you," Hey, you're damaged goods, you don't deserve any better." That voice, **your very own voice**, that justifies that is all you are worth? I've been there and done that!*

‿◠

Words of encouragement

Normal doesn't need to explain itself. But dysfunction does—it needs to justify itself. We humans breathe and bleed the same. You have inherent worth and dignity and you are deserving of respect. You are one of a kind. You are irreplaceable.

Grandiosity says, "Pretend who you are not, and then put on your masks."

Identity speaks, "I am who I am in confidence with a God (Ezer) esteem!"

Courage says, "Look fear in the eye, take it by the horns and speak your truth to it. It is forced to dissipate forever. Let go and let God be your Help (your Ezer)."

Rejection says, "You are not good enough."

Fear says, "Live in a straight jacket."

The thing is, fear doesn't stand a chance when we live in our new identity of how God sees us. Self-doubt and fear need to be thrown in the backseat. Strap them down with a five-point harness and you take the driver's seat.

"She is clothed in strength and dignity and she laughs without fear of the future." —Proverbs 31:25 (NLT)

Brave is not a feeling, brave is an action. Brave is wounded woman to healed warrior (Ezer).

Conclusion to Part III - Broken Identity

W*e carry home in our brains, bodies, and minds, and we carry home in our will and in our emotions. As I have shared my story and evidence from research, it becomes clear that our early attachment histories get wired into the DNA of who we are. We are neurobiologically wired to carry these relational blueprints with us. That means both positive and negative histories including attachment dysfunctions and losses had set up their own highways of neurological circuits, which I learned before the age of two and were reinforced into my adulthood.*

In this section, you read about my clean-up effort of the mess and the damage that it caused. Yes, it is a fact that these acts, attitudes, and afflictions may affect everyone differently and not evenly. Some of us act out, turn inward, become peacemakers, pleasers, or even the "good child." None of us are immune or scar-free. Our traumas impact our lives, work, and play. They steal our health, our emotional, spiritual, relational, and social connection to others, and our creativity. During my awakening, I came to realize these impacts on my life. I have shown you my efforts to overcome these impacts on my life.

Every one of us has a story. We, humans, are stories with a soul. In every story, there are defining moments

211

when change happens. And these moments shape who we are. If you're alive, you have survived something. In this fallen world, we have either gone through something or are going through something. If you haven't, it is just a matter of time. That is the reality of this fallen world. I am grateful for the physical and financial needs my parents provided—the basics of life, my education, etc. Without such support, I would not be here today. This book is not to take away from all their sacrifices and what they did for me. But I know their residual wounds and unresolved past traumas bled all over my life. There is no denying traumatic events are part of the human existence.

We have a choice: we can live in the story of our past, or we can own our story and write a new script. Psychiatrist Dan Siegel reminds us that, "What is shareable is bearable, and what you can name you can tame."

~☺

I looked to the Lord a year after I hit ground zero, the year I turned forty-one. And I felt like I was standing up again. On my birthday, I wrote it out on paper (40 + 1); I was finally standing up like the number 1 in my equation. I thought of my mother deeply. That same day, I received an email from my mother via my father's email account asking, "Have you been searching for me on the internet?" I saw this vision of myself standing up from the ground from this pit of dysfunction. Daddy was obviously disabled from his brain tumors and neurological disease. He could not write or speak. I had been searching for Mom all these years—literally searching for meaning in this relationship. As I sat in bed pondering this email, God divinely and strongly tugged on my heart and soul, ministering to me about his **Mother's Heart**. *He downloaded to my soul a peace I had never experienced before.*

The next few chapters are about what he downloaded that night—that God was with me as my mother, my Mama-G (God), and that he has been carrying me through all these years. It wasn't in my idea or plan to journey through my mother-wounds; however, I would not trade these experiences that I have shared with you regarding what I learned about God's maternal heart for me. I want to share the mother-heart of God that I discovered through the pages of scriptures, through the women who continue to be the image bearers of his maternal love, care, concern, and defense of the defenseless.

Welcome to the next few chapters—the mother-heart of God. Let's dive in.

PART IV:

∽

THE
MOTHER-HEART
OF GOD

215

Introduction to Part IV

"He loves His children with a patient love; a
faithful, fierce, and intimate love. A Womb-love."

—Rebecca Ashbrook Carrell

W*riting the last few sections of this book has been one*
of the most difficult tasks I've ever undertaken. I
felt the nudge of God and the direction of the Holy Spirit
to write this. I also know that God gave me these specific
chapter titles. But my heart was so disconcerted due to my
own inner, critical voices telling me that I was betraying
the people involved in my story. I was gaslighting my own
self and yet working to hush the loud, fear-inducing, anxi-
ety-triggering, false guilt-tripping voices. As I was contem-
plating what to write in this introduction, my heart felt so
defeated. I asked myself who would want to read the junk
in my life—the first three sections of writing. I thought...
what was the purpose in all of this?

One day, as I was attempting to write this introduction,
my husband offered to drop our kids off at school. On their
car ride, they heard on the radio about God's compassion be-
ing a womb-love. My daughter asked, "Isn't that what Mom
is writing about?" They called me right away and told me
what they had heard. My husband encouraged me to write

the morning radio host and tell her how this blessed me. So this scaredy cat, me, found the contact page for the radio station and contacted her. She replied, "I'm on the air." I wrote a brief testimony and thanked her for sharing her message and told her that I was writing a book. She replied and said, "Wow!! God's timing is amazing!" She asked me to thank my husband for listening, and she told me that I could use her quote in my book. God's ways and his timing are amazing!

A womb-love?

I heard a still, small voice speak to me, "God is a birthing mother who loves me with a womb-love!" And I heard him say to me, "Get up, you weary one, my child. Your soul is tired. You've hit many obstacles and you've fallen down. I'm in it with you on this journey of life. I'll teach you how to hold my hand and walk, but then at times, you will feel I'm letting go so you can learn to walk. Sometimes I carry you in my arms. We will get to the finish line together!"

At that moment, I suddenly had more clarity on what I had written about God's maternal heart for me than I had been writing about for nine months. Rebecca nailed it in one quote: "Womb-love." In this section, I take you through God's amazing maternal love for us, his children. I walk you through my own experiences of motherhood. In those hard and holy mothering moments, he taught me the most about his tender and fierce love for me all at the same time. My experiences of motherhood also gave me a window into my mother's challenges that she faced while mothering. My circumstances were replicating hers; however, I chose a different path. I want to encourage you that this womb-love is available not just for me or her, but for you, too!

Chapter 14

⟋♥

MY
CHAOS COORDINATOR

"…the earth was formless and empty, darkness was over the surface of the deep, and the Spirit of God was hovering over the waters."

—Genesis 1:2 (NIV)

I n this chapter, I will walk you through how the Holy Spirit of God hovered over my life, especially during some very dark years of parenting. In fact, he was hovering over my life from conception in my mother's womb, although I did not realize this revelation until much later. My confusion was so dark I did not see any light. There was nothing to separate my dark. In Hebrew, the Holy Spirit is referred to in the feminine pronoun. This was God's rhema word to me, the Word that came alive in my heart that brought light to my darkness.

❧

I sacrificed all the professional ladders I had climbed to be a full-time mommy to my little girl. I dreamed of having a daughter, and I believe that was God's first step in letting me see clearly that this was in his greater plan for redeeming the void of my mother-daughter relationship.

I became the mother who committed all my energy to my first-born child. After a very difficult pregnancy, she was a miracle child. It made it all the more precious to be a mother. My daughter began to get very sick early on, just like my brother had in his childhood. I thought back to the times my mother would care for my brother. However, I was determined to handle this differently. I wasn't going to worry like her.

My baby girl got worse by the year, until one day, after nine months of off and on pneumonia and several months of antibiotics and steroids, her specialists told me she needed to be tested for Cystic Fibrosis (CF). This illness was traced in my family line, and I was committed to doing whatever it took to care for my little one. We followed up through blood work, genetic testing, and spending all the resources we didn't have to find answers. For the first time in a long time, I felt like God finally answered a prayer by providing negative test results and sparing her from CF.

As I expected, the maternal side of my family, including my mother, compared me to my mom's situation with my brother's illness. My situation was minimized by many on my maternal side when I saw them or spoke to them. They didn't closely know our story (no big deal at this point) but I still worried about them. I was always defined as the stay-at-home mom wasting her time, paying too much attention to her child. I did everything I knew to keep her alive and breathing. I didn't need anybody's approval or disapproval.

She is a precious little girl who is caring and sensitive and has had to fight through so much. Like me, she too began to question why she was born, but for different reasons. She was chronically ill, couldn't run and play like her peers, nor was she growing like those around her. My heart grieved for her. I had experienced similar thoughts when I was her age. Something in me wanted to fight for her as well as for myself. My mom made comments like: "I hope you're an excellent mother." "This is too much attention and time you're spending at home; don't you have better things to do?" "Don't waste your time or your life!" "Go get a Ph.D. and get a teaching job at a university rather than sitting at home!"

It sounded like I was sitting in the bathtub all day sipping chamomile tea and popping bonbons. Mother also told me she had always wanted to raise us, but we were stolen from her by circumstances and people who stood in the gap, particularly my paternal grandmother.

As my mother continued to influence the same mindset on my daughter, and my maternal aunts continued to display the same sentiments they had about me toward my daughter, I began to keep them all at arm's length. I stopped responding to their phone calls, text messages, and emails. I did not see anything worthy in their continued demeaning and jealous mentality. I was done with obligatory, mothering relationships.

∽

I was curious to see what God said about *mothering* in scripture. I investigated the scriptures and began to look for the feminine, motherly attributes of God. I was pleasantly surprised to see the mother-ness of God displayed right from the beginning of the creation story in the book of Genesis. If God carried such qualities, then I was determined to explore this. Could God bring order to the inner chaos that was created from my mother-wounds?

When we look back to the creation story in Genesis, we see the Holy Spirit hover over the water. In Hebrew, the grammatical gender of the word "Spirit" ("ruach") is represented in the feminine noun: "she" hovered over the waters although biblical scholars argue against this. In Genesis 1:2 where the Spirit "hovers" over the "waters," some argue the idea may be God's protective care like in the eagle of Deuteronomy 32:11. The confusion and chaos of my life looked much like when the earthly matter and fluids were chaotic at the beginning of Genesis 1. God's spirit brought order to the chaotic, dark, mixed-up world in my unconscious mind, just as God's spirit hovered over the waters with protective care like the eagle's wings as referenced in Deuteronomy 32:11. This was God's rhema (spoken) personal word to me.

Although some biblical scholars argue against this by taking the stance that God was patrolling against the influence of evil (the "deep" implying disorder, chaos, and evil that opposes God) during his creative work, *rhema* incorporated both of these concepts to me.

I visualized God's spirit separating the darkness I experienced in my past from my present, just like the Holy Spirit separated the deep from the deep.

He called the top firmament the sky and the bottom firmament the water and brought order to the chaos in his creation story. In light of what I had discovered, I invited the Holy Spirit to be my helper, to fill my mother void and bring order to the inner chaos of my spirit and my mind.

∽⊙

Reflection Questions

Have you had a time in your life when the darkness around you was too dark to even consider if any sort of light or hope could seep in?

Have you had a time when the chaos of your life was too much to bear, and there was nothing you could do in your human capacity to bring order to your chaos?

Like me, have you found your own dark world (of despair and disappointments, or fill in blanks) spinning on its axis, creating a vortex—you having no option but to spin along?

Have you felt your heart become so overwhelmed by the darkness around you that you couldn't even see it or name it or pray about it? God's spirit hovered over the darkness of the earth, the chaos and confusion of the earth. He separated the light from the dark. His Words spoke light into being.

◡

Words of encouragement

This same spirit is available to you and me. But you may wonder how I know this Spirit. How do I ask for the Spirit?

All you need to do is ask the Spirit to help you as I did. Are you worried you may not have the right words? You do not even need words. This Spirit groans on your behalf:

" ...the Spirit (comes to us and) helps us in our weakness. We do not know what prayer to offer or how to offer it as we should, but the Spirit himself [knows our need and at the right time] intercedes on our behalf with sighs and groanings too deep for words." - Romans 8:26 (AMP)

This reminds me again of Hannah in the temple. She was so destitute, hope-ridden, and grief-stricken that her human words never came off her lips. Her groans puzzled the priest Eli so much that he thought Hannah was drunk. Can I add that he probably thought, **This woman sounds like she is out of her freaking mind!** *I mean, really, don't you see this scene playing out?*

The Message version of Romans 8:26 says this, "Meanwhile, the moment we get tired in the waiting, God's Spirit is right alongside helping us along. If we don't know how or what to pray, it doesn't matter. He does our praying for us, making prayer out of our wordless sighs, our aching groans. He knows us far better than we know ourselves, he knows our pregnant condition and keeps us present before God. That's why we can be so sure that every detail in our lives of love for God is worked into something good."

∽

Final Note

I began to view the Holy Spirit as my "Paraclete" (helpmate and helper, John 14:16) who came alongside me with "wisdom," which is also referred to in the feminine in the book of Proverbs originally written in the Hebrew language. I found this to be an interesting observation. The Holy Spirit became my wonderful counselor, my guide (John 15:26), and my comforter (John 16:13). When I didn't have words, the Holy Spirit gave me groans to pray (Romans 8:26). The Holy Spirit began to give me wisdom and truth and began to reveal attributes of the mother-ness of God in a way that I had never seen in scripture before, in a very personal, almost tangible way. He became my **Chaos Coordinator**.

> *"I still have many things to tell you, but you can't handle them now. But when the Friend comes, the Spirit of the Truth, he will take you by the hand and guide you into all the truth there is. He won't draw attention to himself but will make sense out of what is about to happen and, indeed, out of all*

that I have done and said. He will honor me; he will take from me and deliver it to you. Everything the Father has is also mine. That is why I've said, 'He takes from me and delivers to you."

—John 16:13-15, MSG

My chaos coordinator is available for you, too!

Chapter 15

~☺~

MOTHER HEN

*"Jerusalem,... how often I have longed to gather
your children together, as a hen gathers her chicks
under her wings, and you were not willing."*

—Luke 13:34 (NIV)

F or those of you who are mothers, do you remember the
times when you were a new mother? I do. I have also been
in the lives of new mothers, sharing practical wisdom and assistance right after the birth of their precious newborn. Those
first few days, no doubt, are incredibly overwhelming. Even
while recovering from a broken body—the pain, blood loss, and
emotional toll—we still provide physical and emotional nourishment to a helpless human being. There is something to be
said about the fierceness and protectiveness of us as moms, even
in the midst of the teary, overwhelming, and sleepless nights.
Such is motherhood, and that desire to protect one's young is
a God-given instinct. This chapter is an attempt to describe this

protective, motherly love God has for us, his children.

Just as a mother with overwhelming protective love, Jesus expresses his protective care for us to be safe. In this context, God is sad over those who have turned away from him; however, the heart of God is yearning like a mother hen to "gather" his children, the way a hen gathers her chicks under her wings. He is like a mother hen who nurtures, protects, comforts, and rescues us, shielding us like chicks beneath the hen's wings.

Jesus' use of the mother hen image is a wonderful reminder of God's love for us. Even though we traditionally speak of God as "father," it is a mother's love that is revealed here.

Despite all our failures and shortcomings, how did God's beloved people miss this kind of insane, protective love, the kind of motherly love he demonstrates here for Jerusalem? A baby chick should be close to her mother in the safest haven, where she is the safest physically. Likewise, we should be close to our Creator, Savior, and Lord. This is where we can find safety, comfort, and love.

Luke 13:31-34 (NRSV):

> *At that very hour, some Pharisees came and said to him, "Get away from here, for Herod wants to kill you." He said to them, "Go and tell that fox for me, 'Listen, I am casting out demons and performing cures today and tomorrow, and on the third day I finish my work. Yet today, tomorrow, and the next day, I must be on my way, because it is impossible for a prophet to be killed outside of Jerusalem.' Jerusalem, Jerusalem, the city that kills the prophets and stones those who are sent*

*to it! How often have I desired to gather your
children together as a hen gathers her brood
under her wings, and you were not willing!*

In this passage, Jesus called Herod a fox. He knew that the
Pharisees were messengers. It is almost as if Jesus gives them a
message and knows they will perform the errand of carrying his
message to Herod: "That today and tomorrow, Jesus is casting
out demons and healing people, making people whole."

As a sign of the kingdom of God, Jesus would continue his
work of healing unto the third day. The Pharisees must have
been overjoyed as they thought, "His ministry will end." Instead,
in this passage, Jesus is foretelling his resurrection. But today,
tomorrow, and the next day Jesus would be traveling since a
prophet cannot be killed outside of Jerusalem. Jesus then begins
his lament for Jerusalem, as Jerusalem conspires with Herod
for Jesus' life. In this scripture passage, Jesus compares himself
to a hen. It is a loving image, but not especially dignified. The
chicken in comparison to the eagle is not a magnificent bird,
especially in her fussy, old, protective element.

Almost everyone who heard him knew how a hen protects
her chicks from predators.

Have you ever seen a hawk go after its prey? I remember
Grandma Sara raised chickens. I have seen the fury of the mama
hen when I tried peeking at her eggs while she was incubating
them. No one dared try to witness her little chicks' arrival into
this world! And then, when she exposes her fragile little chicks
to the world outside, a dangerous world of predators, Mama
Hen is fiercely protective.

The old mother hen is often aware of the presence of the hawk in time to gather her chicks under her wings. She is furious in her fuss, she squawks till her brood is safely by her side, she fluffs out her wings and protects them with her own body. The hawk dives down low and the old mother hen turns her body toward him and shrieks and cocks a wary eye without moving from her children. The predator is thwarted but then comes in again for his prey—her precious little chicks. With fierce determination, she spreads her wings wider to keep her babies under her wings, safe and protected. A third time he dives down only to be thwarted for a final time by the determined self-sacrifice of the mother hen. She is too big to be the hawk's target and her chicks are too safe to be seized away. So, he has no option but to fly away. You get the picture.

Another common predator of hens and chicks are foxes. Jesus was trying to protect Jerusalem, but, unfortunately, they rejected Jesus in favor of Herod the fox. Jesus is warned about his death; however, Jesus continues into the city. He will not avoid his execution. What a beautiful picture and imagery Jesus gives us! Jesus has the same care and fierce determination to safeguard Jerusalem. Jesus wants to protect his children ("of Jerusalem") from Herod the fox.

Jesus is like the ultimate mother hen. He moves toward the authorities, and toward conflict. Like the mother hen, he will gather, support and protect his children through thick and thin.

The central theme here is that there is plenty of room for everyone in God's kingdom.

⟋⟍

Reflection Questions

Have you ever considered that a big, holy, authoritative, kingly, majestic God could also love, gather, and protect you under his wings like a mother hen did her chicks?

Can you visualize this metaphor of a mother hen gathering her newborn chicks that God uses to portray God's motherly protective love for us, his children?

Our God is a powerful force, with mighty hands that held the corners of the universe in place. Yet he gathers us, his children, under his protective, motherly wings.

⌒

Words of encouragement

As uncomfortable as it feels to embrace this concept of "motherly love," of God as portrayed in the imagery of a mother hen gathering her chicks, the truth is God loves us with a nurturing, protecting, and comforting love—a Mother-love! I invite you to meditate on this scripture and these attributes of a loving, nurturing, comforting, and protective God as a mother hen does for her child.

Jesus' love can transform all of us and help us on our path to healing. The world should start a movement based on his fierce and protective love.

⌒

Final Note

It is Jesus' desire to gather his children with love and protection in order to draw them closer and closer into his embrace and love. He seeks to include all of his children into the family of humanity that God has intended from the dawn of the Garden of Eden. He ultimately spread out his wings—his hands—on a cross so we could be saved and protected. There is no greater Love than this!

Chapter 16

⌒☉

EAGLE WHO SHELTERS US FROM THE STORM

*"As an eagle stirreth up her nest, fluttereth
over her young, spreadeth abroad her wings,
taketh them, beareth them on her wings."*

—Deuteronomy 32:11 (KJV)

F emale deities were often depicted by birds in the ancient
Middle East. There are traces of this sort of imagery in the
Bible. The Roman Empire exalted the eagle—a strong, powerful,
and mighty bird. In summary, the eagle in ancient times was a
strong bird, evocative of imperial might.

When young eagles attempt flight for the first time, the
mother eagle supports them on the tips of their wings, encouraging, directing, and aiding their feeble efforts toward longer
and effortless flights. In like fashion, God takes the most tender
and powerful care of his chosen people. He carried them out of

Egypt and led them through the wilderness to their promised inheritance. God lifted the Israelites on his wings, like the mother eagle, and he shelters humanity under his protective wings.

Isn't this a beautiful picture of God's mothering love?

I began to see the tender heart of God as my mother. Even in my wilderness, I had not just a heavenly father in my creator, but also a tender, caring, and powerful picture of a mother eagle who carried me through my wilderness. He provided mothers for me in my desperate and most vulnerable desert moments. When my own wings were tired and feeble, he carried me on his wings.

I have a friend and a mother figure, Saley, who has relentlessly dropped everything in her life during times of crisis in mine, showing up every time—for the birth of my children, during my emergency surgeries, and my children's surgeries. She is a mother who stood in the gap and who went to bat for me.

I am reminded of the last time Aunt Saley (I've adopted her as my aunt) was by my hospital bed, responding by quick thinking on her feet— thanks to her extensive experience working in an intensive care unit—as I contended with death. I was reminded of the time my monitors went flat, barely reading a pulse. My son's heartbeat doubled. He was fighting to stay alive inside my collapsing body. And here was a mother with sheltering wings, showing up in the middle of my storm. I made it; my son made it. As I mulled this memory over, I reminisced on God's faithfulness and his unending goodness and love.

All of the times I grieved alone, I didn't have my mother close by to blanket my heart with comfort. There were many roles she didn't fulfill, perhaps some by circumstances, others by choice, but I found a God who is now a mother to me, like the mother eagle, in the absence of my earthly mother. In Isaiah 40:31 (KJV) we read, "But they that wait upon the Lord shall renew their strength; they shall mount up with wings as eagles; they shall run, and not be weary; and they shall walk, and not faint." When my wings were tired from flying on their own, I believe that the God who led the Israelites out of Egypt carried me on his most tender and powerful wings, training me to soar up high with renewed strength in my wings.

~⑤~

Reflection Questions

Do you get the picture of this beautiful and extraordinary metaphor where the female eagle, with extraordinary care and attachment, cherishes her young? Have you ever considered why the God of the Universe would use a metaphor of the eagle, a bird, a created creature of his hands to express his own power, might, and extraordinary care, attachment, nurture, and support?

Why would he explain his imperial might and provide an analogy of fight and flight? Notice this time, it isn't a fight or flight response!

*Have you considered God as someone who **cherishes** you, like the eagle cherishes her young?*

Can you dare to believe that God not only protects, but also cherishes, and loves you with a great attachment like the eagle does for her young? How does it make you feel when you hear God say, "As an eagle stirs up her nest, flutters over her young, spreads abroad her wings, takes them, bears them on her wings." Deuteronomy 32:11 (NKJV)

◠

Words of encouragement

The God of the Universe supports your feeble wings as you take flight from your birth nest (your womb). What an analogy! Like a mother eagle who teaches her young to fly, he teaches us to learn to fly. In this metaphor, the eagle imparts these lessons during flight.

*A mother eagle trains her young in **flight**. This is a flight you can trust unlike the flight to flee. Remember our limbic brain?*

*Researchers have also studied the eagle's fight battles with snakes. Brian Howard writes about this in **National Geographic**; the eagle's strategy is often to tire the snake out until it can strike the reptile in the back of the head.*

> *"The Eagle does not fight the snake on the ground. It picks it up into the sky and changes the battleground, and then it releases the snake into the sky. The snake has no stamina, no power, and no balance in the air. It is useless, weak, and vulnerable unlike on the ground where it is powerful, wise, and deadly. Take your fight into the spiritual realm by praying and when you are in the spiritual realm God takes over your battles."*
>
> —ultrakulture.com

This is such a powerful metaphor of the eagle, it reminds me of Exodus 14:14 (NIV): "The Lord will fight for you; you need only to be still."

❧

Final Note

Naturalists have studied how eagles operate when they see a storm coming. The eagle will fly up very high and wait for the battering winds to arrive. When the winds finally arrive, the eagle will move its wings so the wind will pick it up and lift it above the raging storm. The eagle uses the power of the winds to soar above the storm. The eagle doesn't escape the storm but uses the storm to lift itself higher.

When life's storms come our way, and we trust in God's eagle wings and train dependency on him in the storm, he will renew our strength like the eagle's. We will learn to soar above our life's storms as the winds will lift us higher. When I look back, wondering how I made it, I have nothing else to boast of—only God! Without Him, I couldn't do a thing.

I have seen the turbulent winds of the storms of my life lift me higher. I have overcome the inevitable storms that come to us and have powered through this life only by God's help. And so can you.

Chapter 17

ᦕ

COMPASSIONATE COMPANION

"The Hebrew word translated as 'compassion'
shares a root word with the word womb…"
—Elizabeth W. Corrie
The CEB Women's Bible

I n this particular chapter, I detail an extraordinary loss I
experienced, as well as the grief which accompanied it. The
grief in losing dreams of bringing a baby into this world and
reminders of the broken mother-child relationship that I shared
with my mother were triggered in my deep grief. In my sadness,
I discovered God is a compassionate companion; he cares for
grieving mothers with his womb-love. This chapter is my attempt to show you how my grieving heart met His compassion,
His womb-love.

Picking Up The Shards

⟶

The winds were howling as if the gates of hell had released its shrillest and ugliest cries, with wooing and wailing that chilled to the bone. It was a cold winter morning, after all, and the town had fallen asleep, covered by snow. And yet my insides were on fire, being cut by shards of glassy ice. After a few days of agonizing physical and emotional pain, my husband prayed with me as I laid out my words, my cries, and groans as petitions before God. We believed we were beating the devil out of our home and my womb so that our baby would survive the turmoil on my insides. We had prayed for this child, relentlessly waiting through many infertility treatments, including multiple procedures and surgeries.

Five months prior, on the day of my surgery, I woke up unable to move. My Stage 3 endometriosis had taken over one ovary and twisted it. Due to the weight of the hanging mass, it cut off the blood supply to the one ovary—termed as ovarian torsion. My tubes looked like "sausage," according to my physician. The pictures still give me goosebumps! That surgery, slicing through a massive ball glued to my inner abdominal wall—took four hours, as the doctors cut open my ovaries, scraped and cut through my fallopian tubes, and put all my baby factory organs back in their anatomical positions.

I had put this surgery on the back burner, as my daughter's health took priority over my personal battles. I finally conceived after being given a very "narrow window" after this surgery to mitigate my endometriosis. Even my surgery team was celebrating. And yet, this celebration was short-lived. On this icy morning, I lost our baby girl at the end of my first trimester. (I

242

will write about my pregnancy losses at a later time.)

Suffice it to say, the grief was unbearable. I was isolated. Even worse than what was transpiring in my body was what people said or did to "help me." My Aunt Sissy had disturbing words of stupidity to offer, "It was just a bunch of tissue, you have another child to go to." "It is different from losing a first child."

The same week I was miscarrying and recovering from this nightmare, I got a call from my mother. Daddy had just had a heart attack. Due to lack of medical help in Botswana, where they were living, he had to be medically air-lifted to South Africa, after fourteen hours with a 60-percent coronary artery block. He had been to the only cardiologist in Botswana who had given him blood thinners. At this point, I had just lost my child, and I hadn't disclosed my loss to Mom while my father was suffering a heart attack. As I waited on further news from my mother to know if my dad would make it, I screamed at God. Yes, I did, at the top of my lungs: "You will not do this to me. Do you hear me, God? You cannot take away my child and my father in the same week."

I was so grief-stricken. At this juncture, I got a series of calls from my mother's sisters. Aunt Sissy asked, "Can you give me the phone number to the cardiac ICU? I can't reach your mother." I told her I certainly would not give her the phone number to the nurse's line for emergency calls in the cardiac ICU unit. "What is his blood pressure reading?" "What is his heart rate?" She would educate me on her "cardiology" wisdom. She sounded like ten specialists wrapped up in one degree—an undergraduate nursing degree. I determined I was not going to let the hospital ICU deal with calls from my crazy family or waste precious time that belonged to other patients.

Aunt Sissy continued, "Well, then, I will call you at 2:45 p.m. when you leave work. You can give me all the details when you get home." She decided and assigned me a time when I would be mandated to provide her with information. I was so upset and furious with her. I was dealing with my own body withdrawing from pregnancy hormones, and now back at work trying to hold it together at my job at an elementary school at the time. I told my demanding, insensitive aunt and her husband, Joe, that I couldn't speak to her once I reached home since I had a toddler waiting at the door to be picked up. Uncle Joe said, "You need to go to be with your mother. Get on a plane and go to Washington D.C. You can stay overnight at the Botswana embassy, stand in line, and they will give you a visa. You must go and be there for your mother."

I then called my other aunt and told her I was done talking to all of them. If there were any updates, I would give them to her by email and she could update the rest of the group. I felt like a pipeline through which they could gather and consume information. They weren't the least bit concerned over my dying father, nor were they concerned about me or my intense anxiety about the situation. The only thing they were concerned with was that I needed to be there to "take care of my mother."

I did not travel to D.C. I stopped communicating with this group and eventually applied for my visa online. By the time my visa was delivered, Dad was discharged from the hospital. I did not leave my baby girl behind to go take care of my mom. I supported her through Skype calls and phone conversations. My siblings and other extended family members who resided locally in South Africa were available to support my mother. (Yes, I had siblings already there to help her.)

I was still wallowing in my own grief from my personal loss. My withdrawing pregnancy hormones were spiraling me out of control on a crazy roller coaster ride of emotions. I felt like I was drowning in pain, wondering how I could go on. Jesus said, "… in this world you will have trouble" John 16:33 (NIV).

Maybe you're currently in the depths of your grief, with overwhelming waves of sadness and sorrow suffocating the life out of you. We will all face adversity in this fallen world. We will face the pain of loss, betrayal, and suffering from our own transgressions or sins committed against us. Do we just go on? Do we just survive? Do we cope with what we've learned in experiencing grief to survive? Or do we cope by waiting for the pain to end or survive by numbing out? And if that doesn't work, perhaps even numb our grief with addictions? To be honest, I didn't think I could survive any longer.

෴

In John 16:19-24 (NIV), these were Jesus' words on his very last night before he was taken to be flogged and tortured and crucified:

Jesus saw that they wanted to ask him about this, so he said to them, "Are you asking one another what I meant when I said, 'In a little while you will see me no more, and then after a little while you will see me'? Very truly I tell you, you will weep and mourn while the world rejoices. You will grieve, but your grief will turn to joy. A woman giving birth to a child has pain because her time has come, but when her baby is born she forgets the anguish because of her joy that a child is born into the world. So with you: Now is your time of grief, but I will see you again and you will rejoice, and no one will take away your joy. In that day you will no longer ask me anything. Very truly I tell you, my Father will give you whatever you ask in my name. Until now you have not asked for anything in my name. Ask and you will receive, and your joy will be complete."

Our grief is real. Jesus doesn't deny the degree of pain we will experience.

Great sorrow and suffering are part of this human journey. It is part of our existence in this broken, busted, and fallen world. Our relationships were not meant to be like this! Our Edens were not meant to turn into Gethsemanes.

There was a relational fracture between God and man when sin entered this world through the first humans, our first parents—

Adam and Eve. God's original plan wasn't for you and me to experience this type of grief and loss. I just had to settle in on that truth.

In this passage, God's love is demonstrated even in his grief. His heart aches for us, even like a woman in labor (John 16:21).

God trusted a woman's womb to send his only son who was fully God and fully man to experience the earthly love of a mother. God has a heart that aches and he empathizes with you and me.

Jesus showed compassion to his mother, Mary, and identified with her grieving heart in his dying hour on the cross. He understood his earthly mother's heart was grieving for him, her son, who was just arrested to face crucifixion—the worst possible death. Her emotions at the crucifixion are unimaginable.

In John 19:26-27 (NIV):

When Jesus saw his mother there, and the disciple whom he loved standing nearby, he said to her, "Woman, here is your son," and to the disciple, "Here is your mother." From that time on, this disciple took her into his home.

These are remarkable circumstances of Jesus' death, unavoidable for the fulfillment of the prophecies of the Old Testament. He understands grief. He empathizes with our emotions. He validates the human emotion of grief. Even in his excruciating and agonizing death, Jesus empathizes with the heart of a mother, his mother!

The word "empathize" means to understand and share the feelings of another. Here, Jesus was understanding and sharing the deep, agonizing feelings of his mother. She was about to lose her beloved child, and she wasn't able to help him or do anything in her human capacity to stop the madness of the situation. Christ tenderly provided for his grieving mother's heart. He said to Mary, "Behold my beloved disciple shall be to you a son" (John 19:26). He then gave John, his beloved disciple, the duty to be an affectionate son.

In his last, final dying hours, Jesus empathized with his mother's weakness. He is a high priest (Hebrews 4:15), but he can also sympathize with our weakness. I see Jesus in this picture empathizing with Mary's broken mother's heart over the death of her beloved son. Jesus identifies with her in her pain and secured her an "adopted son." He secured for her a home and consoled her grief by the prospect of sonship by one of his beloved disciples, John.

What a model Jesus provides by sympathizing and empathizing with His mother's heart in her grief while he was in the process of dying, his death making atonement for the sins of the world. Jesus was demonstrating this with the highest degree of tenderness in his most vulnerable and dying hour. He was identifying with the grief of his own mother's heart, reflecting his tenderness through his maternal heart's beat.

In John 16:19-22 (NIV), Jesus saw that they wanted to ask him about this, so he said to them:

Are you asking one another what I meant when I said, 'In a little while you will see me no more, and then after a little while you will see me?' Very truly I tell you, you will weep and mourn while the world rejoices. You will grieve, but your grief will turn to joy. A woman giving birth to a child has pain because her time has come: but when her baby is born she forgets the anguish because of her joy that a child is born into this world. So with you: Now is your time of grief, but I will see you again and you will rejoice, and no one will take away your joy. In that day you will no longer ask me anything!

In Isaiah 42:14 (NIV), God is portrayed with the imagery of being like a woman travailing in childbirth:

"For a long time, I have kept silent. I have been quiet and held myself back. But now, like a woman in childbirth, I cry out, I gasp and pant."

Deuteronomy 32:18 (NIV) states,

"You deserted the Rock, who fathered you, you forgot the God who gave you birth."

This verse refers to the feminine role in the birthing process, and in the Hebrew translation, it not only alludes to giving birth, but to the pain involved. The imagery clearly refers to God giving birth.

Psalm 90:2 (AMPC) states,

"Before the mountains were brought forth or ever, You had formed and given birth to the earth and the world, even from everlasting to everlasting, you are God." The Hebrew translated "you had

formed" means primarily "to be in pangs with child" or "to bear a child." This scripture gives us other hints of the imagery of God giving birth.

Numbers 11:12 (ESV) states,

"Did I conceive all this people? Did I give them birth that you should say to me, 'Carry them in your bosom, as a nurse carries a nursing child, to the land which you swore to give their fathers?"

I can't help but see Moses implying that God has given birth to the Israelites, and therefore it was God's duty to mother them. He is primarily speaking in the feminine with a maternal heart.

James 1:18 (NIV) states,

"He chose to give us birth through the word of truth, that we might be a kind of first fruits of all he created."

In Isaiah, God is like a woman in labor moaning, panting, and gasping. He is in the process of giving birth to his people, and it is not an easy delivery. The birth image continues in the gospel of John as referenced above. Those of us who have given birth, or spouses who have seen a wife deliver, you will have a heightened awareness of the amazing, colorful, yet messy details of what it takes for something to be born. The suffering and the risk involved in birthing for both the one giving birth and the one being born seems to be a pretty good way of talking about God in relationship to the creation and redemption of his people.

༄

Reflection Questions

Is there a time in your life when you were overwhelmed with grief? A grief that seemed to be swallowing you alive?

Do you believe God is in your grief? Is he remote? Would he care enough to understand?

I have asked these questions and I bet you have, too. In your grief, a lot of times, God is the last person you want in your life, because you are questioning him, right?

༄

Words of encouragement

Our grief is real! It is about our losses—of what we had, or what we didn't have, or what could have been. Sometimes it is a loss of our dreams or the little hope we thought we had for a situation. Yes, you are right. Our grief is real and the hope we thought we had can betray us with a different outcome or reality. Jesus doesn't deny the degree of pain we will experience.

Something happens when we acknowledge our grief. As you might already know, we will all go through the different

251

stages of grief; **Denial, Anger, Bargaining, Depression,** *and* **Acceptance.** *It is painful and overwhelming all at the same time. But God has given us emotions to feel and tears to cry. In the story of Lazarus, Jesus was moved with compassion and he wept. We will move through the stages of grief but we are not called to do it alone. I'm here to say, it is okay to grieve, it is okay to feel. Even the God of the Universe did. We are his image bearers with emotions and tears. We need to take time to grieve. The dark clouds will part and the sun will shine again.*

Don't leave your footprints in the sand in the darkness waiting for them to be swept away by waves of sadness. Walk in your footprints and follow the sun (The Son).

Surround yourself with people who, like Jesus, will move into your grief, be in that space with you, sometimes even hold it for you until you can begin to hold some of it yourself. Break your silence, always seek the help you need. And this includes counseling and at times medication. It is not a sin to care for your soul. If self-talk or soul-talk is evil, then King David was possessed.

◎

Final Note

The God of the Universe is a powerful, mighty king, and through Jesus, he reveals his love for us. An all-loving image in the travailing woman is not especially dignified; however, he expresses fragility and provides a picture of vulnerability in order to identify with us.

*When Jesus suffered all these indignities, and finally said, "It is finished," that included unfinished business I had with my mom and the wounding which I had experienced. God's economy often requires breaking before something beautiful is made or birthed. By analogy, once a mother delivers her baby, she forgets the pain of childbirth and embraces the gift of her child. Jesus is available for you, too, to grieve in your sorrows. What breaks your heart breaks his, too. The God who created the Universe and laid the foundations of the earth birthed the seas from its abyss (womb). This same almighty, powerful God is available for you and me with infinite grace and compassion. He is a high priest **who sympathizes with our weaknesses, yet he grieves for us and with us** like a woman going through the pain of childbirth. He sees your suffering. He is in the experience of your suffering with you! So take heart.*

Chapter 18

෧

MOTHER BEAR

*"I will meet them like a bear de-
prived of her cubs..."*

—Hosea 13:8 (NKJV)

The *New American Standard Bible* says, "I will encounter them like a bear robbed of her cubs. And I will tear open their chests; then I will also devour them like a lioness. As a wild beast would tear them."

Do you see our God's protective love and ferociousness, like a mother bear? The bear is a furious creature, as naturalists tell us. No creature loves their young more than the bear. She is fearless and is in dreadful rage when she is bereaved of her young. In this chapter, I want to show you that God's love is fierce for you. He feels emotion for you like a bereaved mother bear who just lost her cubs. "Like a bear robbed of her cubs, I will attack and rip them open ..." Hosea 13:8 (NIV)

This is a passage of scripture that spoke deeply to my heart about the fierce love that God has for me and you. The text presents a picture of God as a ferocious mother bear who has lost her cubs.

⌒

It was just another day in the carpool lane. I picked up my son from preschool and then headed to my daughter's school to pick her up. My child climbed into the car, deep sobs wracking her small body and writhing from the insides of her bowels. I knew instantly that something had gone terribly wrong. I just knew it had to do with the bullying she had been experiencing over the past few weeks.

I asked her what had happened that day. Every ounce of my being wanted to protect her from her pain, invalidated by the adult in the room, her teacher, not believing her and then turning the story around on her. Unfortunately, we had to take the matter to the school's administration, and eventually, there was a resolution. Over time, my daughter was able to forgive her offenders and move forward.

As a parent, I was ready to take on anyone involved, with my *bear* bare hands. My seven-year-old child's "good character" was even blamed as a reason for her being bullied. My goal is not to dignify the bullies by writing this story here, but I wanted to relate my experience with the God of the Universe portrayed in the Bible as a mama bear. You're created in his image. Do you have any doubt as to why you are instinctively ready to fight for your cubs?

The New Living Translation says it this way, "I will tear out your heart," and "I will devour you like a hungry lioness and mangle you like a wild animal."

As documented in the Holy Bible through Hushai's words to Absalom, "Thou knows of thy father and his men, that they might be mighty men, as they be chafed in their minds, as a bear robbed of her whelps in the field" (2 Samuel 17:8).

"Let a man meet a she-bear robbed of her cubs rather than a fool in his folly."
—Proverbs 7:12 (ESV)

She is fierce at all times but becomes even more ferocious when she is robbed of her whelps.

Let's look at the scripture passages together in 2 Kings 2:23-24 (I am not going to focus on the ferocious and graphic descriptions of the attack here, but I want to point you to the fierceness of God):

From there Elisha went up to Bethel. As he was walking along the road, some boys came out of the town and jeered at him. "Get out of here, baldy!" they said. "Get out of here, baldy!" He turned around, looked at them and called down a curse on them in the name of the Lord. Then two bears came out of the woods and mauled forty-two of the boys. And he went on to Mount Carmel and from there returned to Samaria.

This story took place almost 3,000 years ago in the land of Israel. This is not a fairy tale, nor is it a bedtime story we would want to read to our children. However, what happened there a long time ago has something to teach us in the here and now. Elijah was a prophet who spoke the word of God with great power and authority, and he performed many outstanding miracles. One would think Elijah would be greatly loved in his town, but he wasn't.

In contrast, he was horribly treated all his life. He was even driven out of his home and nearly starved to death. A king and queen tried to kill him and everyone blamed him for the trouble their own sins got them into. This man who suffered so much in life was greatly rewarded by God that he went to heaven without dying. When the Lord was through with his work, he took Elijah to heaven in a fiery chariot pulled by flaming horses.

As Elijah was riding into heaven, he gave something to his old friend Elisha, referred to as a mantle. This was the symbol or a sign of Elijah's authority so everyone who saw Elisha wearing it knew that he had Elijah the prophet's power and truth—God's power. Elisha wore the coat and made his way to the city of Bethel. The name Bethel means "the house of God." This is also the place where Jacob had met the Lord a long time before and later where the tabernacle would reside for a long time to come.

You would think the people of Bethel would be the holiest people in Israel. However, that was not the case. They cursed him and did not greet him with kind words. Instead, they made a joke of him. When they saw God's prophet, they mocked him with jokes that were cruel and hateful by saying, "Get out of here, baldy! Get out of here, baldy!" The most offensive comment by far was "Why don't you go up there where Elijah is and just leave us alone?"

When Elisha heard what these kids were saying, he cursed them in God's name. Yes, he did! And two mother bears came out of the woods and attacked those forty-two kids for not respecting the prophet who was speaking God's word. God's word wasn't respected and those kids lost their lives. My point is God is love, and his love for you is fierce. If you stand by his word and are ridiculed for speaking truth, God gets fierce like a mama bear, and he will avenge those who come against his cubs.

I want to encourage you that God is for you and not against you. To those who are mean and ugly to you, please leave the battle in his hands. Don't try to take your own revenge. Our job is to look at our own lives, take inventory, ask the Holy Spirit to speak to our hearts and cleanse us of the things that need settling and order. We can invite him to help us release those who offend us. Leave the rest to him. He is a just God. Justice belongs to the Lord. Let God be God. His love for us is very intense, like the love of a mother bear.

Reflection Questions

Have you experienced pain from abandonment by parents, friends, or by those we work alongside?

Have you experienced abandonment by those whom you have shown kindness to in the past?

∽

Words of encouragement

*I recently sat down with my kids and watched a documentary about bears on the Discovery Channel. After hibernating in the winter months, mama bear and her cubs are on the hunt for food. Although her body is weak from burning all her fat, she is on high alert for signs of danger. Her cubs are her prized possession and priority even as other bears at times seek to prey on her cubs, even though they are of the same kind. Dare someone attack her very own, she is merciless in her defense. Such is God's amazing love for you. His love for you is an everlasting love (Jeremiah 31:3) and he loves **all** who belong to him so much so that he has adopted you into his family with the same fierce intensity of the mother bear.*

*In the end, God wants a relationship with us where we no longer serve out of obedience, but out of love for him which is out of reverence. Nothing can come between God—the mother bear—and her cubs. When mother bear stands up for you, in her ferociousness, nothing can come in the way. Rest in his intense love for you! He is your mama bear and you are his **beloved** cubs.*

Final Note

God revealed to me the fierce nature of His love. His huge hugging bear paws, with a strange fierceness of flaming love and those strong claws, reach out and seize hold of me every time. Drawing us unto him, he embraces us as the beloved ones he has chosen for himself.

He will shear off others who offend us in the process of defending his most deeply wounded—the object of his fierce love. In this biblical account, God didn't cease to devour his scoffers with a tremendous appetite, with violence and desperation. This story, as graphic and uncomfortable as it is, utterly amazes me. The work of his very sharp claws was a demonstration of his *love* in operation for his own that is exceedingly great. His zeal and jealousy are flaming desires that only the divine nature can know. All that matters is that you and I remember that we are mama God's cubs.

The point is God is your mama Bear! Isn't that a cool and amazing metaphor?

Chapter 19

⌒

GOD FAITHFULLY REMEMBERS US

"Can a mother forget the infant at her breast, walk away from the baby she bore? But even if mothers forget, I'd never forget you – never."

—Isaiah 49: 15 (ESV)

"I will never leave you nor forsake you."

—Hebrews 13:5 (ESV)

"I'll never let you down, never walk off and leave you."

—Hebrews 13:5 (MSG)

My paternal grandmother, Sara, was a mother to me like no other. She didn't give me life, but she did stand in the gap, nurture me, taught me things others couldn't even dare teach me. She dressed me, fought for me, held me, kissed me, and most importantly, she loved me *unconditionally*. There are not enough words to describe just how important my grandmother is to me—a mother, the powerful influence that she continues to be—her legacy lives on. I will hold on to that because it cannot be stolen from me. I loved her and continue to love her in heaven. Nobody can put this better than St. Therese of Lisieux when she said, "The loveliest masterpiece of the heart of God is the heart of a mother." In this chapter, I will share with you what I learned about the heartbeat of God's maternal heart to faithfully remember you.

∽

My Grandma Sara would always say that no matter what happened, parents would always love their children. But she really thought of herself that way. She was a very nurturing and loving grandma. She demonstrated and modeled care, concern, and love. She woke up way before anyone did in the household. She started with prayer, then cooked breakfast and lunch, even saving extras just in case an unexpected guest dropped by. Her pot always had rice, vegetables, and curry. She nurtured her children and her grandchildren with her presence, her smile, her embrace, and her stories about the deep things of life. She shared her unparalleled wisdom. She was a great storyteller of history, family, and current events.

My parents provided a roof over my head and did what they could with what they knew. I am grateful for all their investments; however, I experienced neglect and emotional and psychological abuse, as I have recounted. I walked through the first three sections in this book with stories of how I experienced abandonment and neglect from the very people who should have protected me—emotionally and psychologically. I have elaborated on my attachment disturbances, dysfunction, my fear of abandonment, and my struggles to connect.

The only time I remember my mother clearly leaving with her physical presence was on the platform when she left to join my father right before I went to boarding school. I had just turned thirteen. As the train pulled away, I broke off from my sibling, who was also left behind. I was inevitably separated from the youngest who was accompanying my mom. I ran down the platform as if I knew this was it, that the little patches of time living with Mom in a family system was coming to an end. The dream of living together with either of my parents for any amount of time going forward was wishful thinking. I just knew it wasn't coming back.

> *"When my father and my mother forsake*
> *me, then the Lord will take care of me"*
> —Psalm 27:10 (NKJV).

> *"Can a mother forget the baby at her breast and*
> *have no compassion on the child she has borne?*
> *Though she may forget, I will not forget you"*
> —Isaiah 49:15 (NIV).

Yet we see mothers who are mentally ill and abusive, mothers who had a string of live-in boyfriends while growing up, or workaholics who were never "present" and whose work consumed their lives. We see mothers who died from early illness or old age. There is a sting associated with such loss and brokenness in this world.

In this fallen world, no human being is perfect; however, I know we would still like someone whose heart is kind and forgiving, whose generosity comes through and whose shoulders are broad enough, whose strength is unparalleled when we most need them. I certainly do. And I am pretty sure you share my sentiment. We are never too old to desire that connection.

Did you have such a dad, a mom, a caretaker, or someone to stand in the gap for you?

The world seems to be lacking parental devotion, some by circumstances, but others may have actually forsaken their children intentionally. It is unavoidable—abandonment is something everyone has experienced in one form or another. Some of us have experienced abandonment by a father or mother, spouse, boyfriend or girlfriend, either physically or emotionally. Some parents feel abandoned and carry truckloads of resentment toward their children—children whom they've wounded deliberately, intentionally, or sometimes unintentionally. Whether they want to own it or not, they feel abandoned.

People feel abandonment, hurt, or separation by the death of a loved one, even if that death was completely unexpected. People feel abandoned by their employer during the process of "downsizing" or "restructuring" when they no longer have a job. Sometimes we feel forgotten by God.

Once in a while, and nowadays more frequently, we hear stories of a child, a baby abandoned by its parents on the streets, on doorsteps, and in dumpsters. When we feel abandoned by God, the feeling is real. You prayed, but he didn't answer. You read the Bible, but he didn't speak to you. You prayed for the healing of your loved ones, but they didn't get better. Instead, they got worse or even died, and death separated you from them now as a result of God not hearing you.

Trials of life surely made me think that God went on vacation and forgot about me and my problems. Sometimes I even thought he was just too busy attending to someone else, or he was punishing me because I deserved his chastisement. God knows the human situation, whether it is good, bad, mediocre, or outright horrible. He understands the separation. When he had to experience separation from his own son at the cross, it hurt, it stung.

Maybe your parents were different, but even fathers and mothers with good intentions treat their children poorly at times. And sometimes that results in children feeling forsaken, not cared for, or feeling unloved. As we all know, even in the best of families, parents fail. The reality is we all have experienced abandonment one way or another.

For many decades, I experienced insecurity, low self-esteem, a sense of loss and control over my life, isolation, and an inability to focus. I had to come to an understanding that my abandonment experiences were in no way prosecution of my childhood, innate goodness, value, and innocence. Instead, it revealed the flawed, ignorant thinking, false beliefs, and impaired behavior patterns of those who hurt me. The wounds went deep in my young heart and my mind, and real pain was felt.

The pain stayed with me into my adulthood and was a driving force for me to understand and process the reasons for my emotional pain. When I accepted it, I could begin to heal.

Once I got a hold of this truth that God remembers me faithfully and loves me with abandon, I didn't desire or need dysfunctional love. Even if your father and mother forsake you, there is a God who will never do so.

Even if a nursing mother forgets her child at her breast, God will never forsake you. He is the perfect parent and will be the mother and father to you in that void if you let him.

~ා

Reflection Questions

Have you felt abandoned or betrayed by a nearest and dearest friend? A spouse? Abandoned by those you thought were your closest allies? Counselors? Those you could take for their word, yet failed you?

In the fallenness of their hearts, even if they drop you, the love and care of God are far superior to that of the most affectionate relationship that could ever exist. Have you believed God does this for others, yet it is hard to believe this for yourself?

~ා

Words of encouragement

In Isaiah 49:14-15, God saw the sentiment of unbelief and despondency and feelings of being forsaken and forgotten among the children of Israel. God uses the metaphor of a child suckling at his mother's breast and then says that even if she forgets to have compassion on the son of her womb, the child that she bore, that he will not forsake or forget us. He speaks this amazing, mind-blowing statement with the intention of making three points clear:

1. God cannot stop remembering you and me:

*In Genesis 8:1, God remembered not just Noah and his family, but all the animals in the ark. Noah was waiting patiently and obediently for a whole year. And he did hear from God again! The word "remember" is often used in the Bible in the sense of God **taking action** on his promises. He "remembered" Abraham and spared Lot on his behalf (Genesis 19:29). God remembered His covenant with Abraham, Isaac, and Jacob when the Israelites were in bondage in Egypt (Exodus 2:24). God remembered Rachel and she conceived (Genesis 30:22, 23). When God remembers, it points us toward his faithfulness. Although it appears that he has forgotten us or has been silent for a while, he has always proved that he will take action on his promises in the biblical stories, regardless of the time that elapsed.*

2. God cannot stop loving us:

*When David wrote in Psalm 27:10 (NKJV), "When my father and my mother forsake me, then the Lord will take care of me," he used an interesting word. Literally, the sentence means the Lord will **gather** me. Our Savior expressed the same truth when looking at Jerusalem and said how often he would have **gathered** his children together even as a hen gathers her chicks under her wings.*

When family forsakes you, remember Psalm 27 and Isaiah 49. Everything is beautiful about an innocent baby, but there are flawed men and women. Yet God still loves all flawed people including the ones who crucified his son. It defies all understanding when he said to Jeremiah, "... I have loved you with an everlasting love." (Jeremiah 31:3, NIV).

3. God will not forsake us:

Hebrews 13:5 reminds us again that, "Jesus will never leave us nor forsake us."

In Hebrews, Jesus gives us reassuring words of grace for all those who have experienced abandonment in any way or at any level. Some of us have been running down that platform after the train, others have gotten back on the wrong train and ended up right back where we started. We have found ourselves stranded after we've done our best to deny it. Jesus' words to the abandoned and the abandoner remains the same: "I will never leave you nor forsake you." That verse has been true and will remain true forever. Hebrews 13:8 essentially confirms that Jesus Christ is the same yesterday, today, and forever.

271

~ⓢ~

Final Note

Throughout his earthly ministry, Jesus showed compassion to abandoned people who were abandoned by family and friends. Remember the leper and the woman at the well? At the last supper and as his time was drawing to a close, Jesus wanted to make sure they didn't feel abandoned by him, "I will not leave you orphaned." Jesus told them, "I am coming to you. In a little while the world will no longer see me, but you will see me; because I live, you will also live" John 14:18-19 (NRSV).

Later that night after his betrayal by Judas in the garden of Gethsemane, all the disciples deserted him and fled—when Jesus needed them the most. In his final moments on the cross, as he experienced the sting of abandonment, he cried out, "My God, my God, why have you forsaken me?" By his death, he made atonement for both the abandoned and the abandoner, as hard as it is to accept.

That truth sets me free! Remember, Jesus will never leave you nor forsake you, and he is with you till the end of the ages (Matthew 28:20).

Chapter 20

༄

GOD WHO NEVER SLEEPS NOR SLUMBERS

"He will not let your foot be moved; he who keeps you will not slumber; indeed he who watches over Israel will neither slumber nor sleep."

—Psalm 121:3-4 (NIV)

"Every evening I turn my worries over to God. He's going to be up all night anyway."

—Mary Crowley

God gave me the privilege of motherhood to reveal to me what it felt like to not sleep for over a decade now. I am blessed to be in the space of motherhood and believe that the God who never sleeps nor slumbers has got my back in the middle of the night when all seems utterly chaotic. The day will break, and no situation will be forever. I know first-hand what it is like to stay up all night. This chapter is my attempt to show you what I learned about how God is eternally awake, like a mother watching over you and me.

∽

My mother decided to come from Africa during the last few weeks of my first pregnancy. My husband had just returned from a conference out of town and had been offered a job in a different city. I was fully pregnant, due any minute, and I couldn't leave without giving birth. I convinced him that if God opened a door, he should walk through it. Secretly, I wished to get away in hopes of a fresh start. Mom extended her plans to come to stay with me postpartum.

The next morning, I receive a call from her, "I need to go see my mom. My sisters just took turns visiting and have all returned to the U.S. They want me to go because they think she needs to see me right now!" *Well, what about me?* I thought. I was on bed rest, close to giving birth. I was at the doctor's office multiple times a week at this point, as they were monitoring me for preterm labor. Delivering smack dab in the middle of shingles certainly posed the risk of complications for my new baby.

One of my aunts called me to underline it for me; my mother needed to be with Grandma Eli and not me. "People give birth all over the world, including Uganda, and *you* will be just fine," she said. My nerves around my back and my abdomen burned. I had to lie on ice bags lined on the bed and place ice packs on my belly. I felt like someone was skinning me alive. I was consumed by the pain in my nerves. Aunt Sissy called me to offer consolation, "When my daughter was seventeen, she had shingles,"

274

she said. "It wasn't that painful. We brought her home from her dormitory in college and took care of her."

A third aunt called me and stated their mother was more important than me and that's where Mom needed to go and be right now—with Grandma Eli.

Was my mother going to choose all of them over me? What a dynamic; my situation was belittled and minimized. Apparently, I didn't deserve my mom's help or attention. I wasn't their priority. Okay, I agree I wasn't dying, but my husband was going to be away and I was going to be by myself on bed rest. Giving birth in the next six weeks would put the baby at risk for complications per my doctor and being high-risk for preterm labor didn't make it any easier.

What a bind, Lord! Where is Mom? What are you up to, God? Did my mom or any of my other mothering figures care? I asked God if he was asleep. Although I wasn't physically dying, I was suffocating.

I called my Grandpapi and asked about Grandma Eli. He told me that she was stable. "She quit eating for three days due to her Alzheimer's. She is sitting back up in a chair now and wheeling herself around the house. When Pastor Zach came to pray and give her communion, she asked them if they were in a hurry to let her go. She stated boldly that it wasn't her time yet," Grandpapi added. We both laughed. Grandpa Papi told me that Mom's priority should be to be available for me in these last few weeks.

I called Mom. She told me that Grandma Eli was dying and she needed to be there. She had changed plans last minute and she would come after I gave birth. Aunt Sissy called back to let me know that when my mother arrived, she would take her away from me so I would learn how to take care of the baby "myself." She had plans to take her to the Grand Canyon and have her visit her siblings on the West Coast. I told her if that is what she chose, then she should proceed with the plan. She assured me that I wouldn't deliver until she got back from her vacation trip. I thought, *You know, that might just be okay. I might be happier without you here.*

Mom did come, planning to stay with us for a few months. As soon as she returned from her trip to the West Coast, she left with a new job.

How I wished I could get a reprieve from my incessant slumber-less nights. As the weeks went by, I wished my foggy brain would clear. I wanted to shower without worrying about the baby falling out of her swing. I feared if she flipped over, she wouldn't know how to get back on her back and suffocate. How I wished I could just brush my teeth and take a decent shower without worrying about something catastrophic happening. I had no family around to leave my child with. I had isolated myself enough to not have anyone in my life to ask for support. The most I did was step outside for a moment with my baby strapped on me to get a breath of fresh air to my brain. Postpartum blues... they are a real thing.

With my second baby, all day and all night my little guy screamed due to a birth problem that caused him excruciating pain. He was born with a malfunctioning kidney, which resulted in ten months of pain until surgery finally fixed it. Oftentimes, my older child also needed to be attended to all night long. She required around-the-clock breathing treatments in order to stay alive. During those treacherous nights, my anxious heart and eyes watched both my children very closely.

Melatonin and Ambien aided me most days; however, I couldn't depend on medications to either fall asleep or stay asleep. I had to be alert for my little ones. I just wondered if there would ever be any hours in the night when I could sleep without interruption.

These experiences gave me a glimpse into the God of the Universe who never sleeps nor slumbers. I had a profound appreciation for this powerful imagery of God watching over us, not blinking an eye on his beloved children!

With deep admiration, he is protecting us with unwavering love. God is watching over us, his beloved children.

In Psalm 121:3-4, the Psalmist writes, "He will not let your foot be moved; he who keeps you will not slumber; indeed he who watches over Israel will neither slumber nor sleep." At the outset of this song, a weary David looks boldly to the Lord who made the heavens and the earth for help. This was a song of clarity and strength for me in times of uncertainty. It gave me a fresh new perspective with added significance as a new parent who found sleep elusive and fatigue commonplace.

ᴑ

Reflection Questions

Is there a time in your life that you recall when sleep felt elusive and impossible?

Perhaps a time in your life when you couldn't shut an eye all night? Maybe this was during your parenting years? Or maybe during the time you had to care for a loved one? A disabled or chronically-ill child like I did? Or maybe you have been caring for an elderly parent?

Was there a time in your life where you literally felt you couldn't do one more day of life, perhaps due to your health condition and the pain you were enduring, both mentally and physically?

⟨⟩

Words of encouragement

God is eternally awake and limitless in His strength! Think about that for a moment. It is recommended that adults get at least seven hours of sleep or more each night. For parents with newborns, infants, or toddlers, this is a dream. I still dream of the night that I can get seven hours of sleep! God Almighty has an eternal reservoir of strength that our mortal supply cannot compare to. He does not faint. God doesn't need the recommended seven to nine hours of sleep or rest before he is rejuvenated to begin the next day. He is available every minute, every second of every day for all our lives into eternity.

God alone renews our strength (Isaiah 40:31) to parent another day. We all need rest for the body and mind, but he does not faint or grow weary (Isaiah 40:38). And if we go to the Lord asking for rest in our souls, he has promised that very thing of rest and sleep (Psalm 127:2) in a supernatural way to take on the challenges of parenting. He knows; it is in his nature, his DNA, to stay awake eternally!

Final Note

And knowing that, when I lay my head down I can rest in peace. Because God watches over our comings and our goings, as soon our head hits the pillow. Since God never sleeps nor slumbers, even to the smallest degree, we need not be afraid of any harm befalling us while we are asleep.

Man sleeps. A sentinel may slumber on his post by inattention, by long continued wakefulness, or by weariness. A pilot may slumber at the helm. Even a mother may fall asleep by the side of her sick child. But God is never exhausted, he is never weary or inattentive. As Albert Barnes puts it, "He never closes his eyes on the condition of his people, or on the wants of the world."

Chapter 21

⟳

GOD SINGS OVER YOU

*"Your God is present among you, a
strong Warrior there to save you."*

—Zephaniah 3:17 (MSG)

*"...He will rejoice over you with glad-
ness, He will quiet you with his love, He
will rejoice over you with singing."*

—Zephaniah 3:17 (NKJV)

Z ephaniah was a minor prophet God used to bring his message to the people of Judah. As a call for repentance, he
exhorted the people of Judah to consider their wrongdoings,
and he told them of God's displeasure with them because God
passionately loved them. Yet in the middle of their difficult
emotions and circumstances, God also delighted in them. Ironic,
right? When God cleans house, including clearing out relationships or unkind and hurtful things in our lives, he does it with

great, passionate love. Sometimes he changes the people in our lives or our circumstances. But most of all, he changes us as individuals. He quiets us with his love and sings over us with delight when we turn our hearts steadfastly toward him.

I remember the times I continuously held and rocked my colicky first baby in her first ten weeks of life. She would scream every night beginning with the hours of dusk into the early hours of dawn. I read up and tried everything I knew to soothe and comfort her. I frantically talked to other experienced moms, utilized all their wisdom, including rolling my baby up in a "miracle blanket" and putting my infant tummy to tummy for warmth in case my body heat could calm her down. I put my child in a car seat and held it on top of a running clothes dryer for vibrations. I used a swing I had researched and hunted down from a second-hand store. You name it, I tried it, including white noise and music. If you've experienced a colicky baby, this might sound familiar.

I even remember singing, humming, and making "S" and "Z" whooshing sounds to replicate the noises of the womb. Well, I did everything I could to calm my sweet, innocent infant who was helpless to do anything in her own power to calm herself in her distress.

One early morning at 2:00 a.m., I remember putting her in her car seat and driving down the highway, all the while singing and humming and lullabying.

You've seen countless mothers singing over their newborn, rocking, humming, and paying undivided attention to babies in their distress or otherwise. Sometimes after toiling through the hours of the night, all I knew to do was sing over the baby, trying to soothe her with my voice. Then I would hold her and rock her.

On this particular night, a wave of depression moved over me and a sense of defeat was upon me. I was experiencing postpartum blues, alone and stuck at home with a helpless baby. As a first-time parent, the last thing on my mind was being with God alone. But God brought to my mind this verse; Zephaniah 3:17 tells us, "The Lord our God is with us, He is mighty to save us. He will take great delight in us, He will quiet us with his love, He will rejoice over us with singing."

I knew *God* was mighty to save, but what profoundly hit me was this thought, *The God of the Universe who created me also took great delight in me.* What?!?! God takes great delight in me? But not only that, he also promised me that he would quiet me with his love. When waves of depression crashed around me, I was swallowed in the darkness of my fear. Yet his words of promise ministered to me.

I visualized God singing over me, quieting me with his love, wiping away my tears as a mother rocks and sings over and rejoices over her babe.

Through functional MRI studies, neuroscience researchers confirm that when we literally visualize positive protective and nurturing experiences or recall someone in that space including the Divine, our limbic systems calm down.

David in the psalms is documented to have sung to God—a lot!

In Zephaniah 3:17, God explicitly sings over us with delight.

Whatever turbulence occurs within us, for reasons we don't understand, we need to be quieted. God's love will quiet me. Sometimes that means sitting still and meditating on God's love, as a baby in her mother's arms. I visualized him singing over me continually as I worshiped, listened, and quieted down in his presence.

Zephaniah 3 recounts God as a singer. The first half of verse 3:17 describes God as a faithful warrior, the imagery of an immense protective warrior God. The second imagery reflects God's love as a mother for her child, looking at her baby with great delight and singing over her infant to comfort the crying child. Isn't that the cry of all our hearts, to be comforted? With us in mind, God composes a song and sings it intimately to us, not just the duty of merely calming our fears but also providing us with this picture of a joyful parent, specifically, the picture of a mother singing over us.

Hush little darling don't you cry
Mama's gonna sing you a lullaby
And when that lullaby is through
Mama's gonna stay right here with you.

And if you wake up in the night,
Mama's gonna make everything all right
Hush little darling don't you weep
Mama's gonna stay here until you sleep.

There is such incredible intimacy and tenderness in the sentiments displayed in this lullaby. I can't begin to imagine God's tenderness that comes through his promises. He comes to us and quiets us with singing.

Reflection Questions

Have you felt guilty or unworthy of celebration during those early parenting years or any time in general?

Have you struggled with being delighted in by God or others?

Has anyone celebrated you recently?

Words of encouragement

God invites us to cast our worries upon him when we are weary and heavy laden with care. What better cause for our singing and rejoicing than God's singing over us! Just like my baby in my arms, comforted by my singing, let's sing in the knowledge that when we are humble and broken, God's promise to us is to quiet us with his love.

Who knows more about this than the God of the Universe who was rocked in the arms of a peasant girl from Galilea, whom no doubt sang to him, Baby Jesus. This God kneels down and picks us up, wipes our tears, and rejoices over us with singing.

Final Note

Young mothers who are always extending such love to their children also need to be the recipients of such love from God, who is both father and mother to them. We cannot give love to our families if we haven't been poured into by God and others who are the hands and feet of him. **We can only give what we have received**.

~⌒~

Conclusion to Part IV - The Mother-Heart of God

I will never be a perfect mom or a perfect person, but I will live each day with the grace that I am afforded to live. I will reflect the truth that I am an image bearer of God in my motherhood. I have scars from my mother-wounds but I also treasure the overwhelming experience of redemption from God's healing. Our experiences give us the wisdom of what we don't know. God was present in the gaps. He was carrying me in his arms through other women in my life.

You can pause to look in the rearview mirror, take the time you need. I did, and I began to see and celebrate God's maternal heart for me through the inventory of my heart. I took inventory like David and searched for God's maternal heart in scripture. You, too, can share my revelations of God's mother-heart that filled the despair of my mother-wounds. His womb-love is everlasting, and it's limitless; how wide, how deep, how high is his limitless, eternal love.

He who created the limitless expanse of the Universe who laid the foundations of the world, during whose creation the waters burst forth from the abyss (womb) to form the seas, this very same God created you and fully knows you and fully loves you. He is intimately familiar with your form because he created you in the dust of your mother's womb.

He did not need a speck of light because he knew your form, your design. Uniquely and intricately, he wove you together, one irreplaceable special child, one in seven billion. You are fully known and loved by the One who created you and adores you. Just as you are!

In Chapter 1, I called the God of the Universe a liar when he said I was fearfully and wonderfully made. Now I can say he is a truth revealer! I couldn't receive from others or give to others because I hadn't understood the mother-heart of God. Without revelation, there is no redemption. Now I can stand tall with gratitude, in adoration that I am fully known and loved, delighted in and adored by God. David understood this when he said, "For he knows how we are formed, he remembers that we are dust" (Psalms 103:14).

While you wait for morning to break, God breaks through. He gives you a hug while you are waiting in the ache of your heart. He delights in you like a mother gazing lovingly upon her child in her arms. He is a savior, a warrior who is protecting you with a fierce and flaming love, yet also a nurturing, comforting, and unconditional love. In the breaking of your body, in the languishing of your soul, in the traveling pain, and in the indignities of bringing children into this world, a mother is an image bearer of the **One** *who took on everything that was broken in your life to the cross.*

PART V:

❧

CONCLUSION:
MY DECISION

~⑨

Introduction to Part V

E ven those ordinary faults of moms (and dads), the bitterness, and at times, the rage, needs to be released.
It does not depend on the magnitude of our stories for this
is not a competition. These wounds may not have caused
physical death, but they were enough to cause scars that inflicted emotional and spiritual wounds. In this conclusion,
I will walk you through my decision over this mother-child
relationship that was falling to pieces, and how I arrived at
my personal resolution.

Chapter 22

ↄ

FORGIVING
THE UNFORGIVABLE

"Angry once, but no more."

—Anita Oommen

I faced my wounds with the love and support of others; my therapist's support, safe mothers and sisters, in a safe community. God's love and his mother's heart poured into my soul, and I experienced a deliverance deep down in my bones. But I had one more thing to do—forgive Mom and the mothering figures in my life. But forgiveness sounded like a beastly task.

How do I forgive my mother who put me out in the dark at three years of age, with other "mothering figures" sneering and jeering at me for being stubborn?

How do I forgive my aunt who reminded me three decades later at her son's wedding about how "stubborn" my daughter was, just like me?

How do I forgive my mother when emotional, verbal, physical, and even sexual abuse happened to me on her watch? How do I forgive a mother who was not present emotionally, but forced me back to face my abuser with "compassion?"

How do I forgive my Aunt Sissy for calling me names and holding me responsible for my sour relationship with my mom? And how do I forgive this same woman, when years later as I shared vulnerably about my own miscarriage to comfort her as she had lost her grandchild, told me that it was just a "bunch of tissue?" How do I forgive someone who informed me that my sorrow was only deep because I was taking it "too seriously," as I had a living child waiting at home for me to return to? How do I forgive this woman for reminding me that my situation was different and less painful than her daughter's?

How do I forgive my mother and even my siblings who have continued to label me in adulthood as "too emotional," or "having an anger problem?"

How do I forgive Mom who says that my *unforgiveness* has led to all my relational problems in the family? That the health issues I created for myself, my children, and my family are results of my sin?

How do I deal with and process when my mother says anger is silly, that I have a sickness in my bones, and that I don't have a right to my emotions, even as an adult?

Every single time I had a conversation with Mother or my aunts or even my siblings, I would walk away with negative thought patterns, finding myself once again going back to those automatic ways of responding that left me stripped of honor and dignity. I had to take the permission my mom gave away from them. How do I forgive the million times they've commented

292

with sadistic pleasure about my miseries amongst themselves and others? But they are my *family*. I wanted to be deeply wanted, known, and accepted by them.

I had stood up for everyone else and the injustices that were done to them, but I just hadn't stood up for myself yet. How was I to forgive craziness and this *family dysfunction*? How do I, and why should I?

Ultimately, I had to forgive Mom, my siblings, and other family members who had minimized my life, my circumstances, and my pain. They were holding me and my life hostage. Forgiving these mothers and forgiving myself was the next step.

Can we forgive and yet honor our parents?

For me, I had a flood of emotions and confusion as I was working on the forgiveness piece. Even though I had childhood wounds and scars, I was taught consciously and unconsciously that failing to honor my parents was a sin. This is what my mother told me every time I tried to establish boundaries to protect myself from manipulation, emotional and spiritual abuse from the people who had been abusing me. I was disturbed at the idea that I had to honor someone whose actions had been anything but honorable. Did this mean that I had to stay under her control and yield to her manipulations in order please God?

I had to acknowledge the reality and difficulty of my emotions. They were real. I was afraid to face my fears. I had to name and process my emotions. To end my anger, I had to get angry

293

enough to tell myself that I had enough of this vortex, this crazy loop of dysfunction. I had to process underlying wounds of trauma in a healthy manner that included healthy processing of anger and all of the other emotions I had been ruminating on for years.

The Bible says in Deuteronomy (5:16), "Honor your father and mother, as the Lord your God commanded you. Then you will live a long, full life in the land of the Lord your God is giving you."

This was the very verse that my mother used against me to justify that I was abandoning, sinning, and not submitting to her authority and her mothering partners!

The word *honor* shares the same root word that means "heavy." It implies fixing a weighty value on the relationship, on a parent's role in our lives, from a positional standpoint.

But parents *do not* have a right to destroy us or our lives because they brought us into this world. Emotional, physical, verbal, and all forms of abuse are destructive! It is not acceptable in God's eyes or the world's.

After mocking me, my mothering figures always reminded me, "It was a joke." I concluded abuse was no joke, instead, their mockery was evil, dishonorable, and vile.

Even Jesus said in Matthew 10:35-36 (AMP), "I have come to set a man against his father, and a daughter against her mother ..." Your enemies will be right in your own household. Yes, God's word said that!

I had to break this curse, this vicious cycle. As I evaluated my life, I made the decision to honor my parents, my mom, and my mothering figures by realizing "everything" they had done to me and the impact they had on my life. It would ultimately be dealt with. I wanted to own it, then un-own it.

But we don't need to let our abusers manipulate and abuse us in order to please God. We can still choose to love them as we set up boundaries in the relationships. We can best honor our parents by living our lives "worthy of our calling" and by releasing those hurts and wounds. I realized I was holding people hostage in my life, including my spouse and my children. They were held hostage to experience all that brokenness I carried in my life. And most of all, I was holding myself hostage.

The story of the stones

"Let us pick stones out of this basket and write down the names of the people you need to forgive. This is just a visual symbolization of forgiving and we are going to throw these stones into the lake," said my group leader in a recovery group five years ago. I looked around the room. Others in my group were grabbing a couple or three, and then the basket was passed down my way. It was my turn. I picked up seventeen stones. I couldn't contain them in my hand! I had to hold these stones in my skirt and on my lap.

The leader said, "Carry those in your purse for one week and when we come back next week we are going to throw them in the lake!"

Oh, my! My purse was so heavy; however, I followed her instructions and carried my purse around with those stones. By the next week, I was ready to throw *all* my stones. These stones were too heavy to lug around in my purse. It was not worth my energy or time. When the time came to throw my stones in the lake, I kept the stone that represented my mother. I just couldn't throw that one away. I wasn't ready to let it go.

Five years later, I was in a different recovery group, and here we were again; yes, that's right, the act of throwing stones into the lake came up. We had to pick up stones from a basket, write your person on it, and carry it around. This time I carried my stone around, not just in my purse, but wherever I went. I tried to go about my day. I tried brushing my teeth, cooking, and even washing dishes, carrying the dang stone! I even went to communion in church by taking my stone. I tried to pick up the wafer with the stone in my hand. I needed to lay this down at the table, at the "foot of the cross."

It is no surprise that I wasn't able to do much with the hand that I grasped and clenched that stone in. It was time to release this stone that I had been holding onto for dear life. However bitter and angry I was, I needed to let this stone out of my clenched fist into the grace and mercy river of God. I thought about all the myths of forgiveness that I had learned from my own family and even church. Those voices in my head from church and family systems said, "You need to forgive and forget, as quickly as you can. If you talk about any of these offenses to another person you are betraying your own family. Forgive, forget, and move on. You need to be back in relationship with them as soon as possible. That is what a good Christian does."

NO, NO, NO! God never wants us to put ourselves in the way of harm, abuse, and even other people's rage and bitterness. I had to forgive. I learned this very important concept: it takes one to forgive, release, and let go, but it takes two to reconcile.

It goes both ways–it applies to you and the person you are in a relationship with. I was ready to have conversations and take ownership of the way I reacted or responded to my feelings. Unless the offense is acknowledged by the offending party, specifically repented of and the person who has offended you demonstrates with their behavior and actions that they have decided to make a deliberate effort to earn your trust, reconciliation does not occur.

On the other hand, it takes one to forgive. It is a process. Forgiveness does not mean that you are letting your offender "off" the hook. But it does mean allowing the cross of Christ to come between you and the offense. God loves the offender as much as he loves you. His redemption is part of their story, too. Moreover, God is more capable than you are in finding creative ways to deal with the person and what she or he needs to learn from this relational rupture. I learned I could only focus on my choices and responses.

Forgiveness is a choice, not an emotion. Forgiveness is specific and does not depend on the offender accepting or receiving your forgiveness either. By forgiving, you are not approving the offense, minimizing, or justifying what they've done to you, nor are you turning a blind eye by denying what was done to you. Forgiveness is not forgetting, pretending or putting masks on to cover up that you are not hurt. Forgiveness certainly does not depend on reconciliation with your offender.

The truth is that forgiving is hard. But we have to look at the truth. Jesus knows intimately what betrayal is like. If no one else in the world gets it, he gets it! You must look back and address the truth of what was done to you and how it impacted your life. Silencing your anguish or indignation only silences your heart. We must look at the truth of what we know today. Forgiveness takes time; it is a path and a process. We do not need to prematurely forgive; yes, that's right, I just said that! Jesus did not immediately forgive his betrayers. It was later in the midst of his great anguish and suffering that he cried out, "Father forgive them, for they do not know what they are doing."

The decision to forgive is just the beginning of the process. It is simply your agreement to face and examine what the offense has cost you. Like the layers of an onion, each layer needs to be peeled off. We need to look at what it has cost us. Even though we may not be ready right now, what grieved us needs to be looked at and then forgiven. Take all the time you need to forgive.

Ultimately, forgiveness allows us to be set free from the bondage of bitterness and resentment. We let go of the offender's control over us, and we give up the right to retribution for the offense. If we give it all to God, it allows us to become all God made us to be—authentic, free, transparent, and not stuck in the wounds of the past. It releases us from the ruminating, destructive thought patterns that destroy us. It releases us from the victim role and toward freedom. It allows us to take the scab off the wound and allows God to cleanse us. If we keep the scab on and keep applying Band-Aids, the infection only festers and grows, leaking out pus through the cracks usually on to others we love in our lives.

Forgiveness also releases my right to sit in the judgment seat of God. I simply need to return and relinquish my rights to judge my offender. By submitting to God, we are acknowledging his supremacy over our lives and the lives of our offenders—that he alone is God, he alone knows best, and he is the most creative in bringing his sons and daughters to his fold, righting wrongs and bringing healing and justice to all.

Sometimes we need to apply the forgiveness to God and ourselves. I had to forgive God and forgive myself. Forgiveness is independent of reconciliation between two people since it takes two to reconcile.

In Isaiah 66:12 (MSG), the Lord says, "I'll pour robust well-being into her like a river, the glory of nations like a river in flood. You'll nurse at her breasts, nestle in her bosom, and be bounced on her knees. As a mother comforts her child, so I'll comfort you. You will be comforted in Jerusalem."

Amos 5:24 (NIV) states, "But let justice roll on like a river, righteousness like a never-failing stream!"

God extended peace to me like a river. I let all my stones into the waters of his justice and righteousness like an unfailing stream. I did not need to take matters into my own hands. I just had to let go.

Even Abram and Sarai of the Bible, the mother and father of the faith, had brokenness in their relationships. Redemption can happen in spite of *what* we have done. Abram and Sarai left their own country in obedience to walk into the reality of what God had promised them. God, in his infinite and majestic wisdom, gave them the promise of a child. In addition, God would make him a great nation, as large as the number of stars in the night sky. God gave them new names in their new identity, Abraham and Sarah, and even told them what they would name their son—Isaac.

Sarah, by failing to wait and by short-circuiting God's plan, asked Abraham to take another woman (Hagar) to bear him a child. When Hagar got pregnant, Sarah abused and mistreated her maidservant, and Hagar despised her. Once the child arrived, Sarah told Abraham to do with her as he pleased. Essentially, she told him to get rid of the product of her plan. Hagar was sent into the desert with her child. The angel of the Lord found her in her misery on her way to death. She was asked two questions in her dying moment: Where are you coming from? And where are you going?

Even though Hagar despised her mistress, she was hurting and upset to the point that she thought she had no way out but by death. I am pretty sure Hagar had immense unforgiveness in her heart and had no intention of reconciling with Sarah. God showed up right in the middle of her mess, in her pit, with all of the emotions she was battling. I am sure she wanted to die and was okay with her child dying rather than forgiving or reconciling with the family that had put her through so much. God will show up in your misery, even in your state of unforgiveness, to help you. He is merciful; we *can* forgive with his supernatural power, even if we never reconcile!

Chapter 23

Ꮻ

LETTER TO MOM

"Only love can heal the pain that love caused."
—Anonymous

"Love is the answer."
—John Lennon.

You may also be gripped with the question, "Where is Mom?" It has been a journey! I met God in a very special way. As I worked through my own forgiveness, applying the wisdom I had learned and experienced, I realized this core thought: Just as I was formed in my mother's womb by the Eternal One, my creator, so was my mom!

She too was loved by God—a love who is compassionate, intimate, fierce, yet faithful and kind. Only God could drop this thought into my brain.

Both Mom and I shared the following truths, and I found common ground:

- I was formed in my mother's womb.
- I am fearfully and wonderfully made.
- I was hemmed by God in the secret places, and he knows my innermost being.
- He saw me before the earth was created.
- I was created by him by design and for a specific purpose.

So what happened? Why was my mom behaving the way she was and is? Although I found "Mom" in God in and in redeeming relationships, I had always asked this question: What happened to my earthly mom? Was she abused? Was she mentally ill?

Mom, let me start by asking you this question: What happened to you? I understand and know you can only give what you have received or what was modeled for you. I want to say I'm sorry if the things that I experienced happened to you. Something on the inside of you is terribly broken; I have empathy for you. I also have a few questions:

As a little girl, did you dream?

What did you dream?

Who stomped on your dreams?

Was becoming a mother part of your dreams?

How was that attacked or sabotaged?

How did you respond to your void? How did God respond to your void?

God has time and time again proved himself to be faithful to mothers. He saw Hagar in her misery, and he saw Hannah in her desperation and woe on her path to becoming a mother. Bathsheba birthed the man with the greatest wisdom recorded in the Bible out of her betrayal and circumstances. God came through for the widow who tended to the prophet Elijah. If the

God of the Bible sustained them and came through for them in their emotional, physical, and circumstantial pain, he can and will for you. He sustained the orphaned, the abandoned, and the widow. God's heart is for the broken-hearted, and he binds up wounds, including abandonment and rejection traumas. Jesus himself gave his mother a balm for the loss she was going to suffer.

Mom, if you feel that you have lost your children — take heart. Jesus in his dying hour grieved for his own mother's heart. Jesus is grieving for you, too!

Mom, did your mother or others in your life fail to nurture you as a child? Did you find a void, a hole in your heart, that you were looking to fill that no one really ever did?

Did you experience abandonment, neglect, or hurt in your life from your own mother?

If so, how did you experience abandonment from your mother? In turn, did you feel abandoned by God?

Did you fear someone would find you out in your heart's cry?

If you expressed yourself or how you were feeling, did you fear rejection, in knowing and being known?

Were you sapped of emotional energy? Did your marital pain and marriage problems make you feel like you were being torn apart?

Did no one validate you for *who* you were? Instead, did people always give approval based on *what* you *did*?

Whose image are you bearing? A wounded warrior? What parts of God's character were stolen from you? How can they be restored?

I want to let you know that if no one ever understood you or ever walked in your shoes to understand what that feels like, I can tell you that I do. I understand what it must have been like to be a mother of young children with all that chaos going on in your life. It was my chaos, too!

It is my call to action to try to understand what really happened to you. If all of this led you to believe that you were the only one going through all of this, I can tell you, you are not alone. I want to offer you truth in trying to answer my own "why." I want to tell you that what was done to you cannot be excused; however, we have a responsibility to face it, own it, grieve it, forgive the unforgivable, and move forward. I do not want to continue as the "black sheep" of the family, but I want to be a truth teller and want you to receive my truth.

This is a fallen world and in our fallen-ness, God's redemption is still possible. The word "redeem" in Greek means to relieve from the power of another. And that's what I am doing, but you can, too! Mommy, one day, maybe one day, you can begin to love the little girl in you who was ignored and see yourself as a daughter. Then, you won't need those codependent relationships to define who you are, or what your worth is.

Something is terribly broken inside of you. I am so sorry if you were neglected and if your mother was not present. Was she worried about the many things in her world that maybe her life was too overwhelming? Were you scattered? Did you feel like you were losing control? I am sorry no one ever showed you how to take ownership of yourself, your things, or your unique qualities. Did you ever feel worthy of ownership of your own life? You have always said you gave away all your belongings and valuable things to your sisters, whom you treated like daughters and who replaced me. In turn, please don't hate your daughter because I am separate from you. I pray you will find that brokenness repaired by the Repairer of the Breach. He has a mother's heart for you.

Your mother's heart felt betrayed along the years when you felt others, including Grandma Sara, took us away from you. Nobody took us away from you. We have always been your children all along the way. I am truly sorry if you felt that I have not lived up to your "wishes" and "desires."

I pray that you can find the mother-heart of God as I did, that healed my mother-wounds. I want to point you to the mother-heart of God that I've discovered. You have the comfort of his maternal heart available to you! He is a repairer of the breach (Isaiah 58:12). I am breaking the curse by addressing my own wounds and inviting you into this healing journey, which is possible for you, too.

But you have a choice. A choice to heal, to look inward, to take inventory of your life, your childhood, and your emotional, physical, and spiritual health. You have the choice to acknowledge and own and release yourself from the bondage of your past as well. Forgive and repent of your sins of omission or commission, as I did. But if you don't choose this, I am okay to move on in this life in forgiveness of you, yet without reconciliation, in order to move forward in my life.

God is no man's debtor. He desires restoration for you and me and "reconciliation" of this mother-daughter relationship in a healthy way. But we all have individual choices. And I choose life!

The grave, the dust of the womb that I was created in, doesn't hold me down any longer. I am standing up, out of the pit, with a smile on my face, dancing my Irish dance over the mud-covered pit of my past mother-wounds. I am dancing on the plains, the valleys, and the mountain tops!

"Where O' death, where is your sting? Where O' death where is your victory?" Those lines of that song are stuck in my head.

I am alive, I am alive!

Today, you can make a choice! You, too, can choose life, healing, and dancing!

⌣

Final Note

I finally did make the long-awaited trip to India with my family. My beloved Dad passed away a week before our scheduled trip to visit him. It felt like the rug was pulled from under my feet a little too soon. I wish I could have put my hand in his one more time and given him a hug to say goodbye. I took the time to say my farewell by his casket, reminiscing on the handful of precious times I got to spend with him. Although the purpose of this trip was to bury my dad halfway around the globe, I did reconnect with alienated family members in my story with the radical grace that God bestowed upon me. Circumstances could have been better for a family reunion, but in God's Sovereignty, he makes no mistake. He gave me the assurance that he was with me, that he continues to be with me now and he will be with me for eternity.

God's **mother-heart** *embraced mine as I sat by my father's casket, grieving with my earthly mother by my side. Grief and gratitude, pain and compassion for my mother, were dancing together in my heart. Going back to my roots and seeing family I was alienated from for many years was both painful and life-giving in many ways. My heart was wild with gratitude for beautiful moments. I'm so glad I got to write about and process a lot of my pain and hurt from my early years before I made this trip.*

My journey is not over. Do you want to know more about my emotional healing and my broken life restored? Be on the lookout for Books 2 and 3. I will be writing about the life and legacy of my father, titled In my **Father's Heart** *and my life* **Beyond Mother (and Father) Wounds**.

Follow my life story of personal growth and transformation from broken to restored (living in the serendipitous moments of God's grace) at:

https://brokenliferestored.com

https://facebook.com/authoranitao/

https://instagram/authoranitao

Acknowledgments

My greatest desire in writing *Picking Up The Shards* was to give those who have experienced the deep pain of mother-wounds voice to their story by giving words to mine. I wrote these words first for myself—staring fear in the eye, embracing vulnerability, and facing the sting of rejection, abandonment, and isolation that ate at the core of my personhood for many decades of my life.

To my writing coach, Marcy Pusey, thank you! I would not have completed this project without your relentless support, encouragement, and belief in me. Rachel McCracken and Qat Wanders, God put you in my life. Your fingerprints and your heart for me dance all throughout this book. My SPS tribe, you have taught me so much. You are my forever people!

Writing this book has brought a depth of healing to my soul that only my creator God could have made possible! I wouldn't trade any of my experiences, as difficult as they have been, for anything else in this life. God never left my side, nor did he ever leave me orphaned. God is a father and a mother to me—*my best Mom forever*.

So much love to my family who supported me wholeheartedly in this project even when I doubted my own sanity. I thank God for my Grandma Sara. Surely God's goodness and mercy follow me all the days of my life because of her godly wisdom, influence, and the decades of her sunset years she poured into my life.

I chose to write this book by raw authentic processing, with the help of many people God placed along my life's meanderings. I thank God for all the godly women who have mothered me, who model womanhood, motherhood, authentic and genuine relationships worthy of my trust.

Love to dear friends Kelly, Leslie, Amy, Kirsty, Michele, and Tiffany. The impact of your friendship on my life is immeasurable. Ryan, Christine, Gail, Suzanne, Caralisa, Amanda, and Siobhán, thank you for believing in me and this book.

Sarah, your love, laughter, and sisterhood are gifts beyond measure.

My women (Bible study, recovery, and support group) friends, you are my *special* blessings, I love you so much!

Scott, Kerstin, Annie and Debby, thank you for being a safe place for my heart to land.

Melissa, you are truly an amazing friend. Thank you for cheering loudly as you watched this story unfold.

My spiritual mentors who span the globe and decades of my life, thank you for welcoming me into your families and your homes with unconditional love, grace, and acceptance.

To Bijo, thank you for stepping into and embracing me in my then imperfectly, less than, lonely, and left-out life. I love you!

My children, Alaina and Ian, who allowed me space and the time to make this dream come true—you make my life rich and meaningful with heart-bursting amounts of love!

To everyone who picks this book up, thank you! You share my mission in making the world a better place. I hope you will pass the gift of this book forward to someone who needs transformation and healing; from broken to restored.

BIBLE
TRANSLATIONS CITED

◦◦◦

Scriptures

Following are key scriptures that have ministered to me and are referenced throughout this book.

> *"You hem me in behind and before, and you lay your hand upon me. Such knowledge is too wonderful for me, too lofty for me to attain."* —Psalm 139:5-6(NIV)

> *"But whoso shall offend one of these little ones which believe in me, it were better for him that a millstone were hanged about his neck, and that he were drowned in the depth of the sea."* —Matthew 18:6 (KJV)

> *"Before the mountains were born or You gave birth to the earth and the world, even from everlasting to everlasting you are [the eternal] God."* —Psalm 90:2(AMP)

> *"For he knows how we are formed, he remembers that we are dust"* —Psalm 103:14(NIV)

> *"For my thoughts are not your thoughts neither are your ways my ways,"* declares the Lord. As the heavens are higher than the earth so are my

ways higher than your ways and my thoughts than your thoughts." —Isaiah 55:8-9(NIV)

"So God created mankind in his own image; in his own image God created them; He created them male and female." —Genesis 1:27 (ISV)

"A time for everything; For everything there is a season, and a time for every matter under heaven…a time to heal, a time to break down, and a time to build up…" —Ecclesiastes 3:3 (ESV)

"Finally, brothers and sisters, whatever is true, whatever is noble, whatever is right, whatever is pure, whatever is lovely, whatever is admirable—if anything is excellent or praiseworthy—think about such things." —Philippians 4:8 (NIV)

"She is clothed in strength and dignity and she laughs without fear of the future." —Proverbs 31:25(NLT)

" …the earth was formless and empty, darkness was over the surface of the deep, and the Spirit of God was hovering over the waters." —Genesis 1:2 (NIV)

" …the Spirit (comes to us and) helps us in our weakness. We do not know what prayer to offer or how to offer it as we should, but the Spirit Himself [knows our need and at the right time]

intercedes on our behalf with sighs and groanings too deep for words." —Romans 8:26 (AMP)

"Meanwhile, the moment we get tired in the waiting, God's Spirit is right alongside helping us along. If we don't know how or what to pray, it doesn't matter. He does our praying for us, making prayer out of our wordless sighs, our aching groans. He knows us far better than we know ourselves, he knows our pregnant condition and keeps us present before God. That's why we can be so sure that every detail in our lives of love for God is worked into something good." —Romans 8:26 (MSG)

"I still have many things to tell you, but you can't handle them now. But when the Friend comes, the Spirit of the Truth, he will take you by the hand and guide you into all the truth there is. He won't draw attention to himself, but will make sense out of what is about to happen and, indeed, out of all that I have done and said. He will honor me; he will take from me and deliver it to you. Everything the Father has is also mine. That is why I've said, 'He takes from me and delivers to you.'" —John 16:13-15 (MSG)

"Jerusalem, …how often I have longed to gather your children together, as a hen

gathers her chicks under her wings, and you were not willing" —Luke 13:34(NIV)

"At that very hour, some Pharisees came and said to him, "Get away from here, for Herod wants to kill you." He said to them, "go and tell that fox for me, 'Listen, I am casting out demons and performing cures today and tomorrow, and on the third day I finish my work. Yet today, tomorrow, and the next day, I must be on my way, because it is impossible for a prophet to be killed outside of Jerusalem.' Jerusalem, Jerusalem, the city that kills the prophets and stones those who are sent to it! How often have I desired to gather your children together as a hen gathers her brood under her wings, and you were not willing..." —Luke 13:31-34 (NRSV)

"As an eagle stirreth up her nest, fluttereth over her young, spreadeth abroad her wings, taketh them, beareth them on her wings:" —Deuteronomy 32:11(KJV)

"The Lord will fight for you; you need only to be still." —Exodus 14:14(NIV)

When Jesus saw his mother there, and the disciple whom he loved standing nearby, he said to her, "Woman, here is your son," and to the disciple, "Here is your mother."

*From that time on, this disciple took her
into his home. —John 19: 26-27(NIV)*

*"Are you asking one another what I meant when
I said, 'In a little while you will see me no more,
and then after a little while you will see me'? Very
truly I tell you, you will weep and mourn while
the world rejoices. You will grieve, but your grief
will turn to joy. A woman giving birth to a child
has pain because her time has come: but when
her baby is born she forgets the anguish because
of her joy that a child is born into this world. So
with you: Now is your time of grief, but I will see
you again and you will rejoice, and no one will
take away your joy." —John 16:19-22(NIV)*

*For a long time, I have kept silent. I have
been quiet and held myself back. But now,
like a woman in childbirth, I cry out, I gasp
and pant." —Isaiah 42:14-15(NIV)*

*"You deserted the Rock, who fathered
you, you forgot the God who gave you
birth." —Deuteronomy 32:18(NIV)*

*"Did I conceive all these people? Did I give
them birth that you should say to me, 'Carry
them in your bosom, as a nurse carries a
nursing child, to the land which you swore to
give their fathers" —Numbers 11:12 (ESV)*

319

"He chose to give us birth through the word of truth, that we might be a kind of first fruits of all he created." —James 1:18(NIV)

"I will meet them like a bear deprived of her cubs." —Hosea 13: 8(NKJV)

"Let a man meet a she-bear robbed of her cubs rather than a fool in his folly." —Proverbs 17:12(ESV).

"Can a mother forget the infant at her breast, walk away from the baby she bore? But even if mothers forget, I'd never forget you —never." —Isaiah 49: 15 (ESV)

"I will never leave you nor forsake you" —Hebrews 13:5 (ESV)

"I'll never let you down, never walk off and leave you." —Hebrews 13:5 (MSG)

"When my father and my mother forsake me, then the Lord will take care of me." —Psalm 27:10(NKJV)

"Can a mother forget the baby at her breast and have no compassion on the child she has borne? Though she may forget, I will not forget you!" —Isaiah 49:15(NIV)

" ...I have loved thee with an everlasting love ..." —Jeremiah 31:3(NIV)

"I will not leave you orphaned." Jesus told them, "I am coming to you. In a little while the world will no longer see me, but you will see me, because I live, you will also live," —John 14:18-19(NRSV)

"He will not let your foot be moved; he who keeps you will not slumber; indeed he who watches over Israel will neither slumber nor sleep." —Psalm 121:3-4 (NIV)

"Your God is present among you, a strong Warrior there to save you." —Zephaniah 3:17 (MSG)

"... He will rejoice over you with gladness, He will quiet you with his love, He will rejoice over you with singing." —Zephaniah 3:17 (NKJV)

"I'll pour robust well-being into her like a river, the glory of nations like a river in flood. You'll nurse at her breasts, nestle in her bosom, and be bounced on her knees. As a mother comforts her child, so I'll comfort you. You will be comforted in Jerusalem." —Isaiah 66:12(MSG)

"But let justice roll on like a river, righteousness like a never-failing stream!" —Amos 5:24(NIV)

Resources

- https://www.childhelp.org
  The national hotline is available 24/7 at (1-800) 4 -A-child or (1-800) 422-4453.
- https://helpguide.org
- https://preventchildabuse.org/resource/emotional-child-abuse.
- https://www.rainn.org
  You can call the national hotline (1-800-656-HOPE) or (1-800)-4673.

WORKS CITED

Chapter 2. Where Is Home and Where Is Mom?

1. John Ratey, *A User's Guide to The Brain* (New York: Vintage Books, 2001), 227.

2. Ibid. 227.

Chapter 4. Untouched?

3. CDC – Kaiser ACE Study. Retrieved May 19, 2019, from <u>https://www.cdc.gov/violenceprevention/childabuseandneglect/acestudy.about.html</u>

Chapter 6. The Sacred Place

4. My paraphrase of Psalm 139:15.

Chapter 7. Wired for Connection and Created for Intimacy

5. Dennis Coon & John O. Mitterer, *Introduction to Psychology: Gateways to Mind and Behavior*, 12th ed. (Belmont, CA: Wadsworth Cengage Learning, 2010), 48.

6. Ibid. 48.

7. Ibid. 61.

8. John Demos, *Neurofeedback* (New York: W.W. Norton, 2005) 22-56.

9. Louis Cozolino, *The Neuroscience of Human Relationships* (New York: W.W. Norton, 2006), 96.

10. Ibid. 96.

11. Feinstein, Sheryl. *Inside the Teenage Brain: Parenting a Work in Progress* (Lanham, MD: Rowman & Littlefield Education, 2009) 1-6.

12. This paragraph is my paraphrase of Genesis 1:26-28.

Chapter 8. The Power of Touch

13. The University of Washington. "A 'touching sight': How babies' brains process touch builds foundations for learning." ScienceDaily. ScienceDaily, 16 January 2018. https://www.sciencedaily.com/releases/2018/01/180116144027.htm

Chapter 10. Lies Magnified – Who am I?

14. Maria Bogdanos, *Signs of Emotional Abuse*. PsychCentral, 8 July 2018. https://psychcentral.com/blog/signs-of-emotional-abuse/

Chapter 12. Is My Heart at Home Yet?

15. *The New Drama Triangles.* Conference lecture from Dr. Stephen B. Karpman, 11 August 2007. https://karpmandramatriangle.com/pdf/thenewdramatriangles.pdf

16. Stephen Porges, *Neuroception: A Subconscious System for Detecting Threat and Safety*, stephenporges.com, May 2004. https://static1.squarespace.com/static/5c1d025fb27e390a78569537/t/5c-cdff181905f41dbcb689e3/1557004058168/Neuroception.pdf

17. Diane Poole Heller, *Attachment Styles Test.* https://dianepooleheller.com/attachment-test/

18. Dan Siegel, *The Verdict Is In.* https://www.drdansiegel.com/uploads/1271-the-verdict-is-in.pdf

19. Allan Schore, *Affect regulation and The Origin of the Self*, http://www.allanschore.com/booksaffect-regulation-and-the-origin-of-the-self/

ABOUT THE AUTHOR

Anita Oommen has traveled across the globe, from the beautiful continent of Africa to the tranquil villages and bustling cities of India. She currently lives in the U.S.

She is trained as a Speech-Language Pathologist and Audiologist, with dual undergraduate and graduate degrees. She has worked for a United Nations Development Program helping under-resourced and underprivileged children with disabilities. Anita is passionately committed to helping others find their voice—literally and figuratively. She has been equally passionate about her work in neuro-rehabilitation of adults over the last two decades. Brain, behavior, and neuroscience have been her interests. She has also volunteered in the villages and local hospitals of southern India and Africa.

All of her life experiences and the healing that she has experienced have led her to discover that there is no pain too deep, no one too lost that the light of God cannot heal, nor is it ever too late to pick up the pieces of your past and rebuild a new life with resiliency. She is committed to sharing her life story of personal growth and her transformation from broken to restored. Through her writing, she hopes to pass the gift of healing forward and to give a voice to those with similar stories. She writes from her messy dining room table right in the middle of the chaos of everyday life or in her children's school carpool lane when inspiration strikes.

She loves to craft from scratch and enjoys the tranquility of nature, whether it is at the beach, in the mountains, or in her backyard where the skies display God's handiworks.

Anita is a wife to her wonderful husband and a "mama" to two beautiful, smart, and rambunctious children who keep her on her toes. They have taught her to live joyfully and authentically.